Flashbacks

From the Other Side of the Tracks

Gino Carlotti

**Library of Congress
Cataloging-in-Publication Data**

Carlotti, Gino, 1932-
 Flashbacks: From the Other Side
 of the Tracks/Gino Carlotti
 ISBN: 1-893765-02-4 (alk. paper)

1. Regional history 2. Non-fiction 3. Sociology
I. Title. II. Carlotti, Gino

Library of Congress
Control Number: 2001094914

The paper in this book meets the guidelines for
permanence and durability of the Committee on
Production Guidelines for Book Longevity of the
Council of Library Resources.

Published by
Via Media Publishing Company
821 West 24th Street • Erie, PA 16502
E-mail: info@goviamedia.com
www.goviamedia.com

Printed in the United States of America

10 9 8 7 6 5 4 3 2 1
07 06 05 04 03 02 01

CONTENTS

DEDICATION

For
Jessica & Michael
... so they will know a little about their roots.

INTRODUCTION

When Gino Carlotti submitted his first Flashback to me in the fall of 1994, the Flashback column had been a reader favorite for two years. Already, I had a backlog of Saturday morning stories and Gino's submission was tossed onto the stack with the many others.

The Flashback column was a replacement for Larie Pintea's wildly popular "Always Look Back." In mid-1992, after Pintea retired as the longtime managing editor of the *Erie Morning News* and *The Weekender,* I was confronted with filling the huge vacuum left on the page where Larie's column had been. At first, I began plugging the "hole" with wire copy. I asked myself many times: "How does an editor go about replacing the irreplaceable?" How does one replace a classic?

The solution came about by accident. When a reporter wrote a *Good Morning* column much too long for the allotted space, I thought it might work on Saturday's Editorial Page where Larie's column had been. The reporter had written about her early working days at the legendary Marx Toy Company, and, having no idea what to call such a column, I simply labeled it "Flashback."

The next week, another reporter wanted to tell a story about his own souped-up hot-rods of the 1950s. Soon, our readers were contributing as well and I found myself awash in wonderful stories, some dating back to the first decade of the 20th Century, others as current as just a few years ago.

Such was the case when Gino Carlotti wrote his first Flashback. Yet there was something about his work that drew me back to it. His writing style was clear and crisp. It was obvious he was a gifted story-teller. This first submission was about "State Street U," about his working days in downtown Erie during the 1940s and 1950s. It struck a chord with me and I felt it would have a similar impact on many newspaper readers. So I moved Gino's Flashback to the top of the pile, and on Oct. 8, 1994, thousands of readers of the former Saturday *Weekender* learned, or re-learned, about State Street's golden era of retail stores, offices, restaurants, bars and nightlife.

Since that time, Gino, a retired teacher and school administrator, has become the most prolific – and has established himself as one of the most talented – of all the many Flashback writers. With nearly twenty Flashbacks in print, his stories – ranging from his parents' roots in Italy, to Erie's own "Little Italy", to World War II, and the many years in between – have over the years delighted Erie newspaper readers.

Today, the Flashback column has become a classic of its own, recently recognized with an award from the Erie County Historical Society – in no small part because of the literary efforts of Gino Carlotti.

This book is a compilation of Gino's Flashbacks about his family and friends during an historical era many Americans hold close to their hearts and consider the most precious of their lives.

I have enjoyed reading this work every bit as much as I enjoyed Gino's Flashbacks the first time around. What's more, I know you will, too.

Jeff Pinski
Reader Advocate Editor
Erie Times-News
August 2001

PREFACE

The first of my Flashbacks was published on October 8, 1994 and the response I received in the following days was most gratifying and totally unexpected. People called me, sent me notes, or went out of their way at church, at the supermarket, at the mall, and other such places, just to tell me how much they enjoyed reading the article. The second Flashback followed three months later and the response was the same. By the time the third one appeared on June 10, 1995, I was hooked.

Eventually the writing of these articles began to follow a pattern: I would get an idea for a topic, write it, revise it, find an appropriate picture to accompany the article, revise it again, submit it to the Erie Times-News, and then wait to see if it would be published. When it would finally appear in print I would say to myself, "This was the last one – there are no topics left to write about". But four or five months later another idea would crop up and the pattern would be repeated. By May 19 of 2001 eighteen Flashbacks had appeared in the Erie's Saturday morning paper.

One day, after several of the early articles had appeared in the paper, Frank Christoph, an old friend and fellow retired Millcreek teacher, said to me: "You are the only guy I know who is publishing his life's story one chapter at a time". At the time I laughed his comment off as a joke, but as the number of published articles began to increase, I came to realize that what Frank had said might very well be true. With that realization came the thought that it might be wise to keep the entire collection of articles in one place in some kind of logical sequence to pass on to my son and to my grandchildren. Although I had placed an original newspaper copy of each article together with appropriate snap shots in individual file folders, I knew that was really not the best way for this emerging family history to be kept for posterity. File folders just wouldn't do. There had to be a better way.

This book was the answer.

Now there is just one thing to be added to make the collection of these Flashbacks complete and that is to include words of acknowledgement and appreciation to those who have made it all possible. First and foremost, I thank my wife Ann for her patience over the past seven years as I worked on the articles themselves and more recently on putting them together for the publication of this book. She knew how much fun I was having.

Next I thank my son Rick for his valuable critiques. Sometimes his criticisms stung a little, but ultimately I would accept his suggestions because they indeed always made the articles better, as did the technical assistance provided by my old friend Vera Marini Payne. As a former English teacher her private tutoring on grammar and structure were most welcome. I only hope I learned my lessons well.

Thanks to Jeff Pinski of the the Erie Times-News for his encouragement and support in this endeavor and for providing me and the other Flashback writers with the wonderful experience of actually seeing our efforts in print. We were only amateurs but he made us feel like winners of a Pulitzer Prize. And a special word of appreciation to Michael DeMarco for his vision and optimism in regards to this project and for so effortlessly guiding me through the publishing process.

Finally, I must acknowledge all those family members, childhood friends, classmates, old neighbors, former colleagues, and acquaintances who made me feel that writing these articles was a worthwhile endeavor. To those of you who shared my experiences and were part of my life I owe a great debt of gratitude for you truly helped in making this book possible. Grazie.

And Frank Christoph, you were right after all. This is the story of my life.

Gino Carlotti

GROWING UP ETHNIC ~
A WONDERFULLY RICH EXPERIENCE

Those of us who grew up in homes where a language other than English was spoken know what it means to "grow up ethnic". The food our mothers cooked was different from that of our school friends and we had different customs and traditions. All of which contributed to a "we/they" mentality. In my case the "we" were Italians. "They" were everybody else, the Americani.

In fact, I grew up thinking there were only two nationalities in this country — Italians and Americani. Occasionally some non-Italian might be identified as Germanese or Tedesco (German), Polacco (Polish) or even Irlandesi (Irish). We knew the Germans and the Irish had been immigrants too, but because they had been here longer they were already "Americanized". And that is exactly what we wanted to be, Americans, like them.

Our parents were not opposed to these aspirations. In fact, they encouraged our becoming Americani by stressing the importance of going to school, learning the language, being good citizens, and protecting the family's good name. We were not, however, to forget that we were Italians too.

This picture was taken in January 1932 on the very day my parents arrived in Erie from Italy. Standing from left are: my father and mother, Bruna Cavallini, and my aunt Katie. The children in front are my cousins Ednamae (age 7) and Carl (age 5). Bruna, the daughter of my father's cousins Florinda and Virgiglio Cavallini became my godmother when I was baptized later that year.

9

To be sure we became good citizens there were certain values stressed in our upbringing to keep us on the straight and narrow. To label these values and explain them to non-Italians is difficult because they were taught to us through the use of Italian words and phrases that lose a great deal in the translation to English. The words (and facial expressions that often went with them) were the ultimate tools that controlled us and eventually made us the Americans we wanted to be.

Take the phrase *che vergogna* (kay ver-gon-ya) for example. The literal translation is "what a shame". In English that phrase is neither harsh nor threatening, but in an Italian home it meant real trouble. If you did something bad and your mother or father found out about it, all they had to say was *che vergogna* and you were destroyed. If you broke a school rule and got into a little trouble it was *che vergogna!* If you were caught smoking in the alley behind the garage, *che vergogna!* And when your sister was seen holding hands with a boy the family didn't even know, *che vergogna!* You had dishonored the family name. You were a disgrace to all Italians. Where was your pride? Where was your self respect?

Another phrase that was used most effectively was *che peccato*, "what a sin". This one, however, had two meanings, one good one bad. The good one meant sadness or pity. Somebody came down with a terrible sickness, *che peccato*. A man died and left a young wife and children, *che peccato*. The bad meaning, the one used to lay a real guilt trip on a person, had a slightly different connotation. If you did something that earned a *che vergogna* that was one thing, but a *che peccato* was worse. Here you had offended God Himself. You were worthless, lost, doomed. There was no hope.

The interesting thing about these phrases was that a lot depended on the facial expressions and tone of voice used when saying them. When spoken softly with a slow shaking of the head they meant compassion and sympathy. If they were said with a scowl and a low growl it was trouble. For example, if your next door neighbor's wife ran away with the plumber, for the poor husband it was *che peccato* said in a soft caring way. For the wife it was *che peccato* said with loathing and disgust. Actually, for everybody involved (including the plumber) it was definitely a *che disgrazia* (dees-grat-zia) situation, an unfortunate tragedy.

Cleanliness and good grooming were important values also. If your room or your house was a mess or if you ever tried to go out poorly dressed or with soiled clothing you would be labeled a *zingaro* (tzinga-ro). And no self respecting housewife would hang out a wash that wasn't sparkling white. After all, nobody wanted the Americani neighbors to think they lived next door to *zingari*.

I had always thought *zingaro* meant simply sloppy or dirty, but during my first trip to Italy I learned the true meaning of the word. There on a street corner one day I saw a woman and her two children in rags begging for money. My cousin just ignored them and after passing them simply whispered *zingari*. Gypsies.

One could also be labeled a *vagabondo*. Although it sounds like the Italian version of a "vagabond," it really translates to a much more negative expression. If you didn't want to go out and get a job or if you just never seemed to take any responsibility for anything, you were definitely a *vagabondo*, a good-for-nothing, a lazy bum. If this condition went on for some time and you seemed to make a career out of doing nothing then it moved up the scale and became a *vergogna*, an embarrassment to your family. It might even escalate to a *disgrazia* depending on the severity of the individual case.

And so it was. With just a word, a look, a tone of voice, messages were delivered. These were judgments more severe than any court would ever hand down. Yet, in spite of all of this negativism, we grew up proud of who and what we were. After all, we had the support of our family and all our *paesani* (pai-zani), the people who came from the same village as our parents or grandparents. This too, the concept of *paesani*, helped to shape our lives.

Many of us who were first generation Americans had cousins, aunts, uncles and grandparents living in Italy, relatives that we had never met. That void was filled by the *paesani* who came into our homes to visit with our parents and who ultimately became our extended family. They spoke the unique Italian dialect of the region from which our parents emigrated and they were frequent guests in our home and we in theirs. From their conversations around the kitchen table we learned the language, the legends, and the history of the places from which our families originated. Their children were our adopted cousins and became our lifelong friends.

We were taught to be proud of our origins. Yes, we were Italians to all the Americani but to each other we were the Toscani (from Tuscany), or the Calabresi (from Calabria), or the Napoletani (from Naples), or the Siciliani (from Sicily). Each of these regions had their own dialect, their own cuisine, their own customs and traditions. Within regions there were even differences among the cities and towns. Toscani might be Pisani (from Pisa), Lucchesi (from Lucca) or Fiorentini (from Florence). In my case my father, a Toscano, was also a Bientinese (from Bientina, a small town near Pisa) and my Mother was a Ponderese (from Pontedera, also near Pisa).

These regional differences were considered so important that even to this day whenever two Italian-Americans meet for the first time the first question they ask each other is one that I believe is unique to Italians: "What are you?" If the response is one indicating "the same as you," a special bond is formed instantly. In today's Italy these differences still exist but are of much less importance than they were in the early 1900's when many of our families first arrived in America. In modern Italy the various dialects, the major distinction between the regions, have become less noticeable with better education and the spread of a more standardized language as a result of radio and television. To a trained ear there are still some noticeable accents but in most cases the language has become quite homogenized. The major differences now from one region to another seem limited almost exclusively to the kitchen. In the United States, however, the "What are you" question is still asked.

In 1970, at the age of 38, I went to Italy for the first time to meet my aunts, uncles and the many cousins I had known only from letters and old photographs sent to my parents over the years. It was a wonderful

experience and I felt at home with them immediately for I knew the language, I knew the history, I knew all about these people. I felt I had been among them all my life, and my relatives felt as comfortable with me.

ᕃᕈ Winter of 1936 or 1937 with cousins Ednamae and Carl and our dog "Sport" in the yard of our home at 937 West 20th Street. Across the street directly behind Carl is the Cascade Foundry which burned to the ground in the early 1960's.

12

Pictured here are from left: Dorlinda Pardini and her husband Guido, Noemi Ciacchini, my father, Corinna Tempestini and my mother. These were but a few of the "paesani" with whom my parents spent many evenings together in one house or another. Others who were part of this group included Beppe and Angelina Bertini, Cecca and Ubaldo Ciacchini, and Inez and Beppe Chetoni.

They were most impressed with my spoken Italian. The were amazed not because I was bilingual but because I spoke an Italian they had not heard in years. Here in the 1970's I was speaking a 1930's peasant Italian quite unlike the educated and modern Italian they all now used. For them it was as if they had just uncovered an interesting fossil. They were hearing a voice from the past speaking the Italian of their grandparents with an accent and a vocabulary they themselves no longer used. And most amazing of all, it was being done by an American!

I'm sure people my age of other nationalities have had similar experiences. There are no doubt Polish or German words and phrases comparable to *che vergogna* or *che pecato*. Although our ancestors came from different countries and our languages and customs differ, I am also sure there is one thing on which all of us born of foreign parents would agree: growing up ethnic was a wonderfully rich experience.

• • •

THE MAKING OF AN AMERICAN:
MY MOTHER'S STORY

 This Christmas card was sent by my mother to her relatives in Italy in 1932 when I was six months old. It was the first picture my grandfather had seen of his daughter since her arrival in the United States almost one year earlier. It was also the first picture he saw of his new American grandson.

When I was in the early years of grade school I remember learning to read from "Dick & Jane" books. Although it has been almost 60 years since I did so, I can still recall sitting at our kitchen table in the evening after supper and reading those books with my mother at my side. My teacher had said we should do that. "Practice, practice, practice. Your mother will help you." It wasn't until many years later I came to realize that during those sessions in the kitchen, my mother was not really helping me to learn to read — I was helping her!

My mother's name was Corinna Caciagli. She was born in Calcinaia, a small rural town near Pisa in Northern Italy, the youngest of five children and the only girl. When she was 16 her mother died leaving her to become the woman of the house for her father and four brothers. In the summer of 1931, when she was 28 years old, a friend of the family arranged for her to meet Luigi Carlotti who had returned to Italy for a short visit after having been in the United States for several years. He was not on a vacation trip, he was returning to Italy specifically to look for a wife! They met as planned, went through a brief courtship and were married in September of that year.

Three months later the day arrived when they were to begin their journey to America. My mother recalled that her entire family including her father, brothers, sisters-in-laws, nieces and nephews and an assortment of other relatives all went to the railroad station In the small town of Pontedera to see them off. She remembered thinking at the time that she would probably never see any of them again.

She was on the train and standing at an open window from which she could bid her family farewell when suddenly one of her brothers, my Uncle Gino, put his arms around her neck just as the train began to move. It began to move faster and Gino did not let go, if anything he seemed to hold on tighter. Then, at the last possible moment, he released her.

A short while later the train arrived at the next small town as it made its way to the port of Genoa, and there on the platform waiting for the train to stop was Gino! He had raced ahead of the train on his motorcycle so he could say goodbye to his sister one more time. That scene of them holding on to each other until the very last moment was repeated at this stop too and at each of the next two stops as well. Eventually the distances between towns became too great and the speed of the train too fast for Gino to keep up, so the break was finally made and my mother was off to a new world and a new life.

⤳ This is a picture of my mother's father Giuseppe Caciagli with his four sons taken in the 1940's. From left: Umberto, my grandfather, Gino, Alfredo, and Renato. This was one of the first photographs my mother received from any of her family after the end of World War II.

The memory of that scene haunted her for many years. It was, she often said, the saddest day of her life.

I often wonder what it must have been like for people like my mother and father, people with very little education and very few job skills, to leave their homes, their farms, and all their loved ones behind to move to another country, another continent! How must it have been to be suddenly thrown into a society where you knew nothing about its language, its culture or its very way of life. To do so in the depth of the Great Depression, to boot, must have made such moves even more wrenching.

When my parents finally arrived in Erie in early January of 1932 my mother was three months pregnant. They went to the house at 937 West 20th Street which my father had purchased just a year earlier and in which his brother was already living with his wife and two children. There my mother met her new family, my Uncle Egisto, his wife Katie, an American born lady of German descent who spoke no Italian, and their two small children, Ednamae and Carl. For the next 21 years we would live as one family: two mothers, two fathers and three children.

My mother often spoke of those early months in America. They were not easy. First and foremost, she shared a house with another woman, one that didn't even speak the same language as she, and then there was the adjusting to two families living together. Life was complicated, but somehow she managed not only to survive but to thrive in this household.

During those early days in this new country even simple daily tasks presented constant challenges. When shopping, for example, more often than not my mother would pay for all her purchases with bills because she could not understand American coinage. The result of this practice, she said, was to end the day with a purse heavy with pennies, nickels, dimes and quarters.

Eventually that all changed, of course, but I cannot imagine how difficult it must have been for this young woman to be a wife and mother surrounded by strangers in a country that was completely foreign to her. What courage that must have required. What strength she must have had to cope with the daily problems she encountered. Fortunately she was what we today would describe as a "people person". She had a warm, friendly and outgoing character. Combined with her humor, wisdom, and compassion, these qualities drew others to her.

Lillian Quadri was one of those with whom my mother bonded quickly. Lilli lived just three doors away from us on West 20th street when my mother arrived from Italy and they were to become life long friends. What bound them together were the things they had in common: both were young newly weds; both were filled with self assurance; and both were fiercely loyal to their families. They were also kindred spirits who were in love with life.

‿✿ My mother in her garden together with her good friend and neighbor, Lillian Quadri. Every house on our West 20th Street block had beautiful back yards with well maintained vegetable and flower gardens such as seen here.

Unlike my aunt and two cousins, Lilli was an American who spoke fluent Italian and she, more than anyone else, helped my mother become "Americanized". They went everywhere together: to PTA meetings at Sacred Heart School where Lillie's sons "Dickey-Boy" and David and I went to school; to the countryside to buy fruits and vegetables for canning; shopping; and to various social functions in Erie's "Little Italy". They just enjoyed each other's company.

Lilli also helped my mother secure her naturalization papers and in later years even introduced her to the game of football when they went to watch Dick play for Prep. During the war when we bought our first family car, it was Lilli's husband Al who taught my mother to drive. Several years later my mother repaid the kindness, she taught Lilli how to drive!

That first car, a 1936 Chevy sedan, was jointly owned by my parents and my aunt and uncle but it was my mother who was to become the family chauffeur. On our Sunday afternoon rides we would explore the highways and by-ways of northwestern Pennsylvania trying to find where they led. It was not unusual for the kids and Zia (my Aunt Katie) to become very concerned that we might be "lost". But my mother never wavered, she had a wonderful sense of direction. She came to know her way around better than most people, even those born in this country. She liked that.

When my cousins Ednamae and Carl and I each reached the age of sixteen my mother became the family's official driving instructor. She was our one and only teacher and we all passed the driving test on the first try. Well, I'm not sure now, but Ednamae may have had to take the test more than once. No fault of my mother's, I might add!

Over the years my mother became the virtual head of the family: the one who did the banking, all of the shopping, paid the bills and taxes, dealt with repairmen and bureaucrats, and was the "chief cook and bottle washer". She even had time to become active in her church and the ladies' auxiliary of my father's club, the Nuova Aurora. In addition she kept herself well informed on local and national issues and never failed to vote. My mother took her American citizenship seriously.

When I graduated from college and was about to go into the service, it was my mother who said she would take care of my car while I was gone. And take care of it she did. She sold her own car and drove mine for the whole two years that I was gone! This little Italian lady who at that time still wore her hair tied back in a bun, who wore no jewelry or makeup, and was usually attired in cotton house dresses, would cruise around town in my red '46 Chevy convertible—with the top down ! Can you imagine?

It was also while I was in the service that my fiance, Ann Ferrare, helped modernize my mother's appearance. Ann got her to cut her hair, go to a beauty shop on a regular basis, begin to wear lipstick and jewelry and to dress more fashionably. When I first arrived home after 14 months in Korea, I couldn't believe the transformation that had occurred. Her hair had whitened considerably and it was no longer pulled back in a bun for it had been cut short and curled. She had on makeup and earrings and a very stylish dress. It was amazing! My mother was no longer a "little old Italian lady" and she loved the changes as did we all.

In 1956 my parents returned to Italy for three months to celebrate their 25th wedding anniversary. Although Italy was where she had been born and raised, my mother said that while there for those many weeks she couldn't wait to come back to the United States. "This is my country now" she said. "This is my home and where I belong".

She had made the transition after all. She had truly become an American.

• • •

⚓ On the back of this 1986 picture of my mother with my son Rick, my mother had written in Italian: "I'm sure you don't recognize me, but it is me with my grandson. With affection, Corinna." She was probably going to send this to someone in Italy but did not do so for some unknown reason.

19

"God Bless America" ~ My Father's Favorite Prayer

Some time ago I wrote a Flashback article about my mother. The memory of my father now demands equal time.

His name was Luigi but to his relatives and friends he was known as "Gigi". He was born in 1896 in Bientina, a small town in the province of Pisa in the region of Italy known as Tuscany. He was the youngest of seven children, five boys and two girls. He had no special skills and very little formal education and for all of his life in Italy he worked as a farmer and as a common laborer here in the United States.

He came to America in the early 1920's and returned to Italy in the summer of 1931 to find a wife. He married my mother in September and brought his new bride to Erie in January of 1932. I was born in June of that year.

Those are the facts.

 𐁜 My father, shown here with me and my mother in the summer of 1934, was a hard working man. When first coming to United States in the 1920's he worked on the railroad laying tracks, then at Griffin Manufacturing, and finally for the City of Erie as a furnace tender at the incinerator plant. He retired at age 65 in 1962.

On the surface it would seem that the man of whom I am writing was not remarkable in any way but nothing could be further from the truth. I remember that at the time of his death in 1982 I said to my son Rick that *Nonno* (grandfather) had not left us with an inheritance of great wealth or a with lot of property or a thriving family business that would be handed down from generation to generation. There was no material wealth here, but he had left us with something much more valuable: a good name and an abiding faith in God.

That good name came from the way he lived his life. He treated everyone with respect, never speaking unkindly of anyone. He loved company and he loved to make people laugh. He was a simple man with simple tastes. He was honest, loving, loyal, trusting, caring, kind and gentle. In short, he was a good man.

If you were sick he came to visit you and he would never come empty handed; perhaps with a bag of plums or figs from one of the trees in his yard, or some tomatoes and fresh lettuce from his garden, or maybe a bottle of his homemade wine. He would assure you that you were going to be just fine and he would pray for you. Believe me, if he said he would pray for you he would pray for you!

If there was a death in your family he would come as soon as he heard about it to pay his respects and he would do so properly attired in white shirt and a black tie. Black ties were an important part of my father's wardrobe. Not only did he wear them for visiting a funeral home or going to a funeral, but he wore them to Mass on the Sunday closest to the

∾ My father enjoyed socializing with his "paesani". Pictured here clockwise from the front: Joe Ciacchini, Dorlinda Pardini, Noemi Ciacchini, Corinna Tempestini, my mother and father, Guido Pardini, Rose Pardini, and Armand "Babe" Pardini.

21

anniversaries of the deaths of his parents or his brothers and sisters. He believed in praying for and honoring the dead.

The thing I remember most about *Babbo* ("father" in the Tuscan dialect) is his relationship with God. Prayer was an important part of his life and although Italian men in general are not known as dedicated church goers, my father was a unique exception. He never missed Sunday Mass. If there was a special problem that needed solving or if there was some special need to be met, Babbo would talk to God and take care of it. He made deals with God. If God granted him his wish, he said, he would promise to do something for God in return.

The best example of this is when I was in the army and was about to ship out for a tour of duty in Korea in 1954. At dinner on the last Sunday before I was to leave for overseas Babbo announced to me, my mother, and my fiance Ann Ferrare, that there was no need to worry. He was sure I would come home safe and sound. After all, he had made a promise to God that morning at mass that if I would not be harmed he would plant a tree in God's honor. Case closed. I would be just fine. He had arranged for my safety.

"A tree?", I thought. "God already has a bazillion trees!"

Well, I did come back safe and sound in the winter of 1955.

One Sunday in the following spring Ann and I arrived for our usual Sunday dinner with my parents when I noticed something unusual. There was a large hole dug in the middle of the lawn alongside the house and a small tree was lying there waiting to be planted. There were also several small American flags stuck into the ground around the hole. Upon entering the house Babbo informed us that before we ate we had to join him in the yard for "a ceremony". There, alongside that hole, we prayed together. Babbo, in his white shirt and coat and tie, thanked God for my safe return and then, as he had promised almost two years before, he planted the tree. God now had a bazillion and one trees.

That was not the only time Babbo put out an American flag. He always, without fail, flew a flag on any day of national significance. He was proud to be an American citizen and he was grateful for what this country had given him. He came here as a poor unskilled and uneducated immigrant and although he had to work hard all his life to provide for his family, he was able to survive the Depression years and eventually own his own home and have everything he needed to be happy and secure. The greatest blessing of all for him was to have enjoyed 20 wonderful years of retirement with not one, but two pensions. One pension was from the United States Government (Social Security) and one from the City of Erie for whom he had worked for many years. What a wonderful country!

Always, upon ending a meal – even a very simple meal – he would put his hands together and say: "*Grazie a Dio, ho mangiato bene* (Thanks be to God, I have eaten well). God Bless America." The last three words were always said in English.

Shortly before his death he was in the hospital and as is the case with many elderly people when they are hospitalized, he became disoriented and confused. When I went into his room for my daily visit he would often think I was one of his brothers. At those times our conversation would be about Bientina, his childhood, and about things I really did not understand. He would talk about the farm where he grew up and he would ask about his mother and father, about neighbors and old boyhood friends. I would make up answers to appease him and he would become very animated and even more eager to talk about his youth. Sometimes he thought he had seen his mother or his father in the hospital hallway that day and that would make him particularly happy. I learned a lot about him and his childhood during these strange but interesting sessions.

One night I was called back to the hospital because Babbo had become very agitated and somewhat violent. He was frightened by the darkness and the shadows in the hallway and he became confused and thought the nurses and the orderlies were going to hurt him. He was shouting and swinging his cane around and keeping the nurses and orderlies at a distance and the noise and confusion he was causing was keeping the patients on the whole floor awake. They had to call me for help.

When I entered the room I was able to quiet him but it took some time before he really began to relax. To help calm him I suggested that perhaps we could pray together and he liked that idea. Although I do not know my prayers in Italian I do know the Hail Mary in Latin, so with the lights out and holding his hand we began to pray. "*Ave Maria, gratia plena dominus tecum . . .*" I don't know how many Ave Maria's we said together in that darkened room that night but eventually he fell asleep. He was finally, truly, at peace. And I had a memory to cherish for the rest of my life.

Babbo loved life. He loved nature, his garden, his fruit trees, his grape vines, and his chickens. He loved everything and everyone. And above all, he loved my mother and his family.

On his tomb stone at Calvary Cemetery are carved his name, date of birth and date of death, the basic facts. Plus there is the imprint of the two medals he was awarded by the Italian government for his military service in World War I. He was so proud of those medals that I am certain he would be pleased they are now a permanent part of his headstone.

I have but one regret, however. I wish I had had his favorite prayer inscribed there too . . . "God Bless America!"

• • •

‿ This is my favorite picture of my parents. It was taken in 1978 at Presque Isle during one of the very few times in his life that my father actually went to the beach. He and my mother often drove around the peninsula just for the ride, but never had a picnic there.

THE SOUNDS & SMELLS
OF WEST 20TH STREET

The sounds and smells of the West 20th Street neighborhood where I grew up remain in my memory as if I had experienced them yesterday. They were the background that added color to our daily lives.

Living just one block from the 19th street tracks, we could hear approaching train whistles throughout the day and night. They blew not only to alert traffic at the railway crossings, but served as a call for mothers to take down the hanging wash before it was covered with soot from the steam engine's coal-burning boilers. Most importantly, they were a siren call to kids who lived nearby to come watch the passing show.

And what a show it was, filled with wonder and adventure. There were trains from distant states made up of coal cars, box cars, liquid tank cars, and cars carrying livestock. Trailing behind these colorful caravans were the ever present red cabooses bearing the trainmen who never failed to wave to us as we stood just yards away from the moving monsters. During World War II there were trains carrying tanks and jeeps and army trucks and occasionally a troop train carrying soldiers off to God-knows-where. Sometimes there were passenger trains with elegant dining cars and people staring back at us from the blur of passing windows.

⌘ This 1933 picture was taken on the pathway that led from our back door to our chicken coop which is directly behind where my mother is standing. That wicker buggy I'm sitting in would be a collector's item today.

25

The box cars themselves were rolling billboards displaying the names and logos of various railway lines from all parts of the United State, and the graffiti scrawled on the sides of those cars was a constant source of curiosity. Could Kilroy really have been in all those places?

Like similar Erie neighborhoods that abutted the industrial areas of the city, our lives were also punctuated by the whistles of the nearby factories. They blew at the beginning and the end of the work day; they blew at the beginning and the end of lunch times. Mothers used these sounds to check the accuracy of their clocks and as a signal to start the kids back to school after lunch. And at midnight on New Year's Eve it was the factories that whistled out the old year and welcomed in the new. The descending ball on Times Square was to come into our living rooms years later.

Bells, too, helped regulate our lives. Although they still ring today, it seems we heard them more often years ago. Catholic Churches rang their bells five minutes before the beginning of masses on Sunday; they called the faithful to pray the Angelus three times a day; they tolled for funerals; rang out in celebration at weddings; and announced the hours of the day. Like the the churches, the bells rung by the watchmen at major railroad crossings also served as an announcement. Here, however, it was to announce an approaching train and to stop traffic.

Along with the mechanical sounds that surrounded us were heard a symphony of voices: mothers calling children from half a block away; kids yelling up at windows, "Hey, Nor-mannnnnann, can you come out and play?"; the screeching of kids playing Red Rover and Kick the Can; farmers selling live chickens, eggs and fresh vegetables from the backs of their slowly-moving trucks; the rag man from his horse drawn wagon bellowing out his "Reggggggs"; and the calling of the knife and scissors sharpener as he made his annual visit through the streets. Our neighborhood was not a silent place.

Other regular visitors along our block included the Fuller Brush man, the Jewel Tea man, and the insurance man collecting his monthly payments. There was a bread man, a milkman, and an egg man, and the mailman who delivered twice a day. Once a week the garbage collector came right into the backyard to empty your garbage can. In winter it was the delivery of coal down the chute into the cellar. (I wonder what my grandchildren would think if they found a ton of coal in their basement today?) In summer the man with his pony came around to take pictures of kids on horseback wearing a cowboy hat and chaps.

26

Mothers wanted the pictures. Kids just wanted to get on the pony!

Yes, our neighborhood was a busy place and the neighborhood dogs barked a lot.

The crowing of roosters was another sound we heard in our little world. This daily wake-up call emanated from the many chicken coops in the alleys that cut through almost every city block. In the alley behind our house there were at least five such coops that I remember: DeSantis', Quadri's, Bevilaqua's, DiMarco's and, of course, ours. Our coop housed rabbits as well as chickens and, until some of the neighbors complained, pigeons as well.

Alleys, what a wonderful convenience! They were short cuts for going to the house of a friend, to school, to the store, or to go from one block to another without walking "out in front". They were a network of unpaved, somewhat secluded passageways that were used primarily by people to put their cars in the garages that faced the alley rather than on the street in front of the house. Alleys were also terrific places to play cops and robbers or cowboys and indians, to hide, and to secretly learn to smoke cigarettes.

No story of what life was like when I was growing up would be complete, however, without remembering the smells that surrounded us! A walk through our neighborhood, especially on the way to church on Sunday mornings, was like a stroll through a gastronomical bazaar. You could tell what everyone was making for diner. In the Italian neighborhoods it was the aroma of pasta sauces being prepared while in others it would be the smell of less familiar cooking: sauerkraut and other cabbage dishes, meats roasting, or soups being made. It all depended on the nationality of the family.

When walking past these houses in late summer and early fall you could tell who was canning tomatoes or who was making wine. Then too there was the smell of the backyard gardens just after the fertilizer had been spread, some of which came from the conveniently located chicken coops. And those who lived near the industrial areas knew the shop smells, too. In our block a lot depended on which way the wind was blowing. Sometime we smelled rubber from the Continental Rubber Works at W. 20th and Liberty or the wonderful aroma of fresh bread from Firch's Bakery at W. 20th and Cranberry.

Yes, sounds, smells and the activities of a busy neighborhood were a memorable part of my growing up years.

What I wouldn't give to again hear one of my father's roosters crowing, or smell my mothers sauce cooking, or climb into a freshly made bed with sheets that had been dried that very day in sunlight.

Oh, how pleasant it is to remember it all

• • •

❧ Just about everybody I know who grew up in the 1930's has a picture like this one. The photographer with his pony came around every summer and kids really begged to have their picture taken wearing the cowboy hat, the scarf around the neck and the white fur chaps. For just a few moments we flelt like real cowboys. Note the tape marks on my left arm – I had just received my vaccination for first grade a few days earlier. This picture was taken in 1938.

Porches:
Box Seats for Life's Parade

ᐱ This is the house where I grew up at 937 West 20th Street. My father purchased it in 1930. According to old copies of the deed, it was originally the farm house of the Brown family after whom Brown Avenue was named. On hot summer days my friends and I would sit on that large porch with its oversize awnings and enjoy the cool breezes that blew across from one side to the other.

My wife Ann and I visited Italy recently, where we stayed with relatives in the small town from which my parents emigrated more than 60 years ago. One of the things we enjoyed most about the time spent there was strolling the streets on the beautiful summer evenings and talking to people who were sitting on their balconies, on their front steps or at their front doors, just waiting to visit with passers-by.

It brought to mind the house where I grew up. It had a wonderful front porch as did everybody else's house in our neighborhood. These were big and deep and in most cases they stretched across the entire front of the house. Some even wrapped around to side doors. Porches helped cool the house in warm weather and protect it from rain and snow in winter, and it was here that we sat on the swing on hot summer afternoons and read comic books. It was here that we played cards and Monopoly. And it was here, in our box seats, that we watched the passing parade of people.

Our house was on West 20th between Plum and Cascade. Although we were an Italian-American family, strictly speaking our little world was not a part of what was known as "Little Italy." We lived west of Liberty Street and south of the 19th Street tracks; we lived in the "Italian suburbs." Like all city neighborhoods back then it was a great place to be and a great place in which to grow up. Everything you needed was within walking distance.

On almost every corner stood a neighborhood grocery store. Because the owners of these stores knew you and your family on a first name basis it was not unusual for them to allow you to purchase groceries on credit. The amount of each sale was written in a small book, and once each week families would go in to pay the tab. At Ferraro and Cutri's where my family did its grocery shopping, we would always get a free half dozen oranges as a bonus whenever we paid "the bill". We also shopped at Merlino's on 20th and Cascade, Bellomini's on 21st & Raspberry (also known as "Occhio Bello's"), and Archie Nero's at Brown Avenue and Plum. An occasional trip to the Central Market at 16th Street between State and Peach was about as far from the corner store as we ever strayed.

A trip today through my old neighborhood still shows the remnants of many of those stores. The buildings are still there but they now serve other purposes: beauty parlors, apartments, and even churches. No longer can kids run down to one of these convenient locations to buy some penny candy.

But stores were not the only business establishments found in our small world. There were also the barber shops, beauty parlors, churches, schools and drug stores. And, of course, let's not forget the bars: Hector's and Luigi's on opposite corners at 18th and Liberty; Lefty's in the 600 block of West 18th Street, and the Menini's Pitt Restaurant on the point at the intersection of 21st Street, Brown Avenue and Plum Street. Add to those the clubs that were nearby: Sons of Italy, Calabrese Club, La Nuova Aurora, the National Club and the "PP" Club.

Amidst all these establishments stood the pillars of our society: St. Paul's Church, St. George Funeral Home, and Columbus School. For those of us in the "Italian suburbs" there was St. Steven's and Sacred Heart churches, Orlando's Funeral Home, and Irving and Sacred Heart schools. Providing critical health services were the neighborhood doctors and dentists all of whom were, by necessity, bilingual. These includes medical Doctors Leone, Trippi, Pistori, Narducci, Scibetta, and DiSantis. The dentists were Doctors Lupino, Grimaldi, and another Narducci. Providing needed translation services, insurance coverage, and guidance through bureaucratic red tape were Mr. Berarducci, Mr. Cappabianca, and Mr. Phillips.

West 18th Street from Liberty to Chestnut was our "mall". It was there we found the Arrow and Colonial drug stores, Spelta's tailor shop, Goldfarb's dry goods store, Vagnarelli's photo studio, Pedano's Flower Shop, a "Five & Dime" variety store, Faulhaber's Furniture, Schwab Wallpaper and Paint, and the West End Hardware store.

While shopping with our mothers we could also check out what was playing at the three neighborhood theaters: the West 18th Street, the Lyric, and the American. Changed three times a week, the features at these theaters ran Sunday and Monday, new ones for Tuesday, Wednesday and Thursday, and still another change for Friday and Saturday. Often times we went to the movies twice in one weekend and since they were always double features it was not uncommon for kids to see four pictures a week. It was at the neighborhood theaters where we learned all about cowboys and Indians and cops and robbers. That was also where we saw what was going on in the rest of the world with "newsreels" and the "March of Time". CNN was yet to be born.

For boys especially, the Lyric Theater on a Saturday afternoon was the place to be. Week after week we would rush to see the next "chapter" in the continuing series. Was Jack Armstrong going to escape? Would the good guys win over the bad guys? Would the hero save the girl? (It was ok if he saved her, we just didn't want him kissing her. Ugh!)

Occasionally we would venture a little further from home and go to the Follies theater at 26th and Poplar or the Hillcrest near 26th and Peach. When we got a little older and especially when we began dating, we came to know the major movie houses downtown – the Warner, the Shea's, the Columbia, the Strand, and the Colonial.

If we weren't at the movies we were at the ice cream parlors: Born's on 26th and Elmwood; Reiger's at 26th and Cascade; the Liberty Ice Cream Bar at Liberty and Brown Avenue; Spath's on Liberty between 17th and 18th; and Henry's in the 500 block of West 18th. We gorged on sundaes, sodas, banana splits, floats and cherry Cokes as we put nickels in the jukebox.

Today, the passing parade of friendly neighbors is no more and the old porches are gone too. When older homes needed to be remodeled their wooden siding was covered with various kinds of shingles or aluminum. It was during these renovations that porches were often altered to create a more modern look. What was once a comfortable, cozy, somewhat private space became an exposed shell. Some porches were reduced to a mere roof over the front door. More often than not, however, the old front porch just disappeared completely.

Ironically, porches are back on many homes being built today. These are long, not quite as deep as the old-fashioned ones, and they are filled with beautiful furniture. But heaven forbid, nobody sits on these porches! They're just there for decoration. And even if you do sit on one of these porches of the '90's, who is there to talk to? Nobody passes by any more except those who are walking or running for exercise and they can't stop to talk.

Today, nobody walks to a nearby store, or to church, or to the corner mail box. Nobody walks to the movies or to the doctor's office or to the ice cream parlor. And certainly, nobody sits on a porch and plays Monopoly.

With all these changes, however, Ann and I are lucky. We get to relive the past every couple of years when we return to Italy and sit with our relatives in front of their houses, on their balconies, or in their gardens to watch their world pass by. It is then that we fondly remember our old front porches back home.

• • •

This is that same house years later after the house had been sided with green shingles and where railings had been added to the stairs leading up to the porch. Not only were the large bushes

in front of the porch removed, but awnings were no longer put up in the summer. Note the size of the tree trunk compared to that in the earlier picture. Both trees were planted at the same time.

"La Zia" ~
My German-American Aunt

She was tall, somewhat aloof among strangers, rather distinguished, I thought, and a wonderful story teller. And she was a very important part of my growing up years in that we lived together in one house for 21 years – she and her husband and two children and me with my parents. Her name was Catherine – "Katie" Sebald Carlotti – and she was my aunt, the one I knew as "La Zia".

✍ This picture of the five Sebald sisters was taken in about 1901 when my aunt Katie was 13 or 14 years old. Standing are from left: my aunt, and Mary Heidt. Seated from left are: Margaret Bambauer, Kunigunda "Kunie" Sebald, and Barbara Ekerman. Together with their eight brothers, they lived at 517 West 17th Street.

La Zia on the steps of our front porch in the 1940's.

That name, or rather that title of "La Zia", needs some explaining. "Zia" means aunt in Italian. When speaking of an aunt in the third person it is perfectly correct to refer to her solely as "Zia" without the first name being mentioned as in "Is Zia at home?" or "Have you seen Zia today?" But add the "la" before the word "Zia" and it takes on an altogether different meaning.

The best way to explain this subtle but significant change is to use Maria Calas, the famous opera singer, as an example. In the world of music – as in other forms of entertainment, sports or politics – referring to a person simply by their last name is quite common. Pavarotti, Garbo, DiMaggio, and Roosevelt are good examples. But in the case of Maria Calas, more often than not she was referred to simply as "La Calas". The addition of that small two letter word which is the article that means "the" turns that person's name into something special. "Calas" would have been acceptable for just an ordinary diva but "La Calas" was someone special, above the norm.

And so it was with "La Zia". She was different. Worthy of a little more respect. She was above the ordinary. She was the one who had to be handled with kid gloves.

So what made her so different, and so special? The main reason was that she was in a house, a family, a community of Italian speaking people and she was not Italian. She was a German-American, born in the United States. She was not one of us. She was "La Zia". That being said, let me tell you a little about this remarkable woman.

She was born and raised at 517 West 17th Street, in a neighborhood that is today still referred to as "Little Italy". But, in 1887 when she was born, the area around 17th and Walnut was not an Italian neighborhood by any means. It was a German settlement. Her parents had emigrated from Germany in the mid 1800's coming to the United States on a sailing ship. They settled on Erie's west side in the small German community among people they knew, people who spoke their language. A look back at the names of businesses that sprung up in that area at the time is proof of that German influence: Hershberger's Bakery, Schwab's Wallpaper and Paint, Schwartz's Grocery Store, and Uhlrich Leather Goods.

Eventually this predominantly Catholic community decided they needed their own church. The German Catholic church of St. Joseph's was just too far away up at 24th and Sassafras. And here is where La Zia would weave a wonderful story about how the German Parish of St. Michael's came to be established.

As she recounted many times, a group of seven men got together one evening and decided they wanted to found a neighborhood church. They began investigating the procedures they would have to follow to get the bishop to approve establishing a new parish on the west side. Once they knew what the procedures would be they began to save the money needed to begin the building of their church.

Keep in mind that these were not rich men. They were recently arrived immigrants or sons of immigrants who were all working class family men. Contributing to the founding and eventual building of a church was going to require a great deal of sacrifice.

Well, they reached the point one day when this new parish-to-be had to have a name. What did the founding committee wish to name it? It was decided that the only fair way was to have every man write his first name on a piece of paper and place it in a hat. The name that was drawn would be the name of the new church. La Zia's father, Michael Sebald, put his name in as did the others. When the name was drawn it was decided – it would be called St. Michael's Church. La Zia was always proud of her father's important contribution to Erie history.

The church eventually established a school in its basement and all the children of the neighborhood attended. Half of the school day was conducted in German and the other half in English. As the neighborhood grew westward and southward, St. Michael's soon spun off parishioners to form another German Catholic church up on 26th and Liberty. That church, Sacred Heart Parish, was founded in 1894. In his history of the Erie Catholic Diocese, "Cathedral in the Wilderness", Monsignor Robert Barcio refers to Sacred Heart Church as the daughter parish of St. Michael's. In fact, when the cornerstone of Sacred Heart was blessed on June 10, 1894, Father Lachermeier of St. Michael's graciously allowed one of his altar boys to serve at the celebration. His name was Vitus

Reiser, a young man who 39 years later would return to Sacred Heart as its second pastor. La Zia knew Vitus Reiser as a boy and she also knew his long time housekeeper, Tillie Kaiser, all of whom grew up in Zia's old German neighborhood.

Eventually Italian immigrants began to move into the neighborhood where they slowly became the majority of residents and in the tradition established by the Germans who preceded them, they too wanted to build a Catholic church to serve their people. Although St. Michael's was already in their midst, it was a German church, and the Italians just did not feel welcome there and so the parish of St. Paul's was born. But that's another story.

At any rate, in the early 1970's St. Michael's was destroyed by fire and among what little could be salvaged were the three large bronze bells from the church's bell tower. As was the tradition in the Catholic Church at the time of the building of St Michael's, the bells were "baptized" and given names before being installed in the church tower. The largest of the three was "Michael" – named after La Zia's father. And where are those bells today, you ask? They hang proudly in the belfry of St. Jude's Church at the corner of Sixth and Peninsula Drive. I never drive by that intersection without thinking of my wonderful aunt.

That story of St. Michael's was just one of the many that my cousins Ednamae and Carl and I would listen to as their mother conjured up wonderful pictures of old time Erie for us. She would tell of how her family celebrated Christmas when she was a girl and how she used to take the "street cars" to get around town and out to Waldameer Park. She told us about the Millcreek flood and how it devastated the downtown in 1915. And she told of how things were done differently in the "old days".

In the stories that La Zia told she used words that became common in our home but were hardly ever used by our friends or neighbors. Characters with questionable backgrounds were "scalawags". If we wanted to refer to something up the block or down the block from our house we said "up the line" or "down the line". And if La Zia wanted to show displeasure with something she would simply say "oh pshaw". Things done quickly were done "lickety split".

La Zia was fun. She taught us to sing and how to tell stories and she made up games that would keep us busy when there seemed to be nothing else to do. In the summer time we would sit for hours on our front porch and listen to her stories and we would "count cars". Yes, count cars.

36

Here is how it worked. You had to pick a direction, east or west, and you counted all the cars going past the house in your direction. If there were more than two of us playing we would form teams and we would see who would get the most cars before it was time to go into the house for bedtime.

Now in those days, before and during World War II, cars passing by the 900 block of West 20th were not that numerous. On a typical summer evening from supper until dark you would be lucky if you counted five or six cars going in your direction. In fact, I used to run off the porch and stand in the middle of street to see if any cars were coming from "down the line". And if there was one, I would want to count it as soon as I saw it in the distance. I wouldn't be allowed to, however. The rule was that the car actually had to pass in front of the house to count. The ones going up Plum or down Cascade Street didn't count either. Oh pshaw!

My fondest memory of things La Zia and I would do together when I was little was to go for walks at night. We would walk all around the neighborhood and if it was cold she would wear her wonderful fur coat and I would keep one hand in her pocket that was lined in satin. It was soft and warm and after a while I would switch to the other side to warm the other hand too. And all the while she would be telling me stories about different people and different events and when we got back home she would make hot cocoa for me before I went to bed. How I enjoyed those night time walks and how well I remember them.

La Zia was a wonderful baker and cook too. She made delicious from-scratch cakes for our birthdays and German cookies at Christmas time. She made the best French Toast I ever tasted and wonderful roast beef with creamy mashed potatoes. Sauerkraut and pork with dumplings was her favorite.

Yes, we were an Italian household and had wonderful Italian meals and traditions but La Zia gave us German and American classics too: lemon, pumpkin and apple pies, custards and bread pudding. We even made our own root beer, canned our own catsup, made chillie sauce, and all kinds of canned fruits and vegetables.

My mother used to tell the story about how when she first arrived from Italy and moved in with my aunt and uncle, my aunt use to cook those wonderful sauerkraut dinners, especially on cold winter days. My poor mother, pregnant with me at the time, had to leave the house because that strong unfamiliar odor of cooking cabbage would make her sick. Strangely enough not only did she learn to live with the aroma, in

37

time she actually became a pretty good sauerkraut cook herself!

How lucky I was to live in this bilingual house where my parents and my uncle spoke Italian and La Zia and my two cousins spoke English. I had the best of three worlds – Italian, German, and American. And when I think of those days growing up on West 20th Street I can't help but remember that wonderful tall lady whom I will never forget, my second mother, my Aunt Katie – "La Zia".

• • •

La Zia with me on the day I graduated from the eighth grade at Sacred Heart School in June of 1946.

TRIGGERING HOLIDAY MEMORIES

It seems the older we get the more we think back to the days of our youth and remember in our mind's eye what life was like "in the good old days". Those thoughts seem to occur more often during the Christmas holidays. This past Christmas was no exception.

One day during my exercise walk at the Millcreek Mall, I glanced in a store window and for just a fleeting moment saw a nativity set that looked familiar. Where had I seen it before? One of the three kings in particular held my attention. His white beard, his flowing robes, the way he bore the gifts in his hands: this was more than just a familiar looking figurine. I knew this king. As I resumed my walk it hit me. The nativity set I had seen just moments earlier was identical to the one we had at home when I was a boy. But how could that be? I'm almost 70 years old. Do they use the same molds today that they used back in the 30's? Under each piece in the set we had, was stamped the words "Made in Germany". I wondered where this set came from.

Now my mind was racing and I was amazed at how well I suddenly remembered that old nativity set in all its detail: the shepherd with a sheep on his shoulder; the shepherd girl carrying a water jug; the black king with his elaborate robes and a colorful turban; the small mirror we placed in front of the sheep with its lowered head so it would look like it was drinking from a pond; the beautiful sheep dog and the kneeling angel.

As I continued with my walk I began to recall more of my childhood at Christmas time. I remembered the trees (big, real ones) with large multi-colored lights, the kind when if one bulb burned out, they all went out, and long hanging metallic icicles. And I remembered that we never had a metal tree stand like those a lot of people used. Instead my father and my uncle would remove several branches from the bottom of the tree so that a long piece of trunk was exposed. This was placed in a large bucket which was then filled with coal. That was it. No nails, no rope, no wires. Just coal in a bucket and the tree stood tall and steady in the corner.

My job, because I was the youngest in the family, was to tend to the nativity set which was always placed beneath the tree. The coal bucket

✿ Rick with my parents and his "Nana", Martha Ferrare, at Christmas 1980.

and the floor around it would be covered with a white sheet and the manger with the figures of Joseph, Mary and the Baby Jesus would be placed at one end along the wall. When everything was in place, we would scatter artificial snow over the entire scene. The snow was shiny, reflecting the lights from the tree. I can still see it!

Each day I moved the figures of shepherds and kings a little closer to the manger, just a few inches each day. By January 6, feast of he Epiphany, the kings would replace the shepherds at the head of the procession. And with the arrival of the kings, Christmas was officially over for another year.

About two weeks before this past Christmas my memory was jogged again. The elementary school my grandson Michael attends sponsors a well stocked "Christmas Store" where the children can do their Christmas shopping for family members. It is all very organized with announced dates when each class is scheduled to shop. PTA moms are there to assist with selections and gift wrapping.

When I went to pick Michael up at the end of school on his "shopping day", he was all excited about the gifts he had bought. He was very proud of the fact that this year he had used his own money to buy gifts for his parents, his sister, his grandparents, and even for his cat. His sister, Jessica, who is in middle school, used her own money on a shopping trip to the mall.

Telling me about their shopping experiences triggered memories of my gift buying days as a child. In my case, however, it was not at a school store or the Millcreek Mall but rather to stores close to home. One year I went to Benedict's at West 26th between Raspberry and Cranberry. Another it was to a "Five and Dime" on West 18th Street between Walnut and Chestnut. And one year it was to a small store on the south east corner of 26th and Hazel across the street from the Folly Theater. The name of that store escapes me, however.

Jim Mayer, a boyhood friend from Sacred Heart School who now lives in Parma, Ohio, said it was a Kresge's Five and Dime when I sent him an e-mail asking if he remembered the name. Two other former classmates, Jean Walker and Jean Weschler, told me it was called Nason & Prittie's. We are not certain of its name, but we all agree the store was there!

I can even remember some of the things I bought during those adventurous shopping trips: a watch fob for my father; a thimble for my mother; a lapel pin for my aunt; some hankies for my cousin Ednamae; a fountain pen for cousin Carl.

For those who may not know what a watch fob was, let me explain. Back in the 30's and 40's some men, especially older ones, carried pocket watches rather than wear a wrist watch. A fob was a small chain or piece of leather or fabric that was attached to the watch and worn hanging out of the pocket. Often times the end of the fob had a medallion or some such ornament attached to it and to extract the watch from the pocket, all a man had to do was pull on the fob and out would pop the watch. Some fobs were attached to long ornate gold or silver chains that when worn with a vest extended across a man's chest from one pocket to another. The fob I bought my father was very simple and not so expensive.

Most of all, however, I remember the feelings I had when doing my Christmas shopping. Like Michael and Jessica, I too was spending "my money" for the people I cared about and I was doing a very adult thing – shopping for gifts all by myself. And they were wonderful gifts, some even cost more than fifty cents! It was all part of the fun of Christmas.

As we were making plans for this year's holiday gatherings my daughter-in-law, Mary, asked what we used to have for Christmas dinner when we were kids. "Did you have turkey?", she asked. My answer surprised her. "No", I said, "we always had a capon". Well, the discussion that followed explaining exactly what a capon is (a castrated rooster!) was most amusing, but suffice to say that she had never eaten such a food. That question, too, brought back a flood of memories.

Christmas always meant having three things we did not normally eat at other times of the year. In addition to cappone (Italian for capon) there were home made ravioli and home made pizzelle ("pizzells" as non-Italians say). We occasionally had ravioli at other times of the year, but it had to be a very, very special occasion for those to be made.

The pizzelle were a really special treat because we only got them once a year and that was primarily because they were not easy to make. Today they are made with electric pizzelle grills similar to waffle irons that make two at a time. Back then, however, my mother made them one at a time with a heavy hinged cast iron device with a long handle that had to be held over the open flame of the stove. It was hard work and a very slow tedious job. But the smell of anise that filled the house while they were being made would linger for more than a day and that aroma became identified with Christmas.

Each year now as we unpack the Christmas decorations and begin to trim the tree I am reminded of the early years of our marriage when our son Rick was a little boy, the time when he was called "Ricky" rather than Rick. What reminds me most of those years is when I see ornaments we bought for our very early Christmas trees over forty-four years ago.

Most of our old ornaments have been broken and are gone now, but we still have a few that trigger memories of our first apartment and our first house. There are ornaments with flocked designs of teddy bears and Santa Claus and ornaments with nursery rhymes and snow men. Because Ricky used to play drums we had a number of ornaments of drums in different styles and sizes. The ones that remain are discolored and faded now, but I remember hanging them on trees gone by, real trees, flocked trees (yes, we bought real trees and then sprayed them with artificial snow), and our very first artificial tree which had branches like bottle brushes. Now that was an ugly tree.

ᕀ Our 1960 Christmas card when Rick was two years old.

〜 Winter fun in 1945. That's me in the back on the left emerging from a snow house we had just built. My friends are Carl "Buster" Minzenberger, Dickey Quadri, and Norman Grode.

And speaking of ugly, I'm glad we never did follow the crowd and buy one of those skimpy aluminum trees. Remember those? Because they were metal you could not hang lights on them for fear of a short circuit so you had to place a spotlight underneath the tree with a revolving disc of ever-changing colors. Oh well, to each his own.

This past Christmas was certainly a white one and the mountain of snow that developed at the end of our plowed driveway reminded me of the fun we used to have after a heavy snowfall. We would spend hours rolling snow into huge balls. The balls would get so large and so heavy that we couldn't move them any farther beyond a certain point. Some became giant snowmen while others became walls for a fort or a snow house. Forts were great places to hide behind during a snowball fight. Sometime we would even build two forts and have a war! Talk about fun!

Maybe I just don't look in the right places, but it seems to me that kids don't take advantage of the snow like we used to. Do kids make angels in the snow anymore? If you don't know what those are ask any-one in the "Senior Citizen" category, they'll tell you how to make them.

So it was this past Christmas. Everything around me brought back thoughts and feelings of days gone by. They were good, happy memories and all it took was a little snow, a discolored ornament, and a king from a nativity set.

• • •

UNPAVED STREETS

When our son Rick was a small child (he is now over 40!) he asked me one day if the streets of Erie were paved when I was a boy. My first reaction was to remind him that I was born in 1932, not 1832. But the truth is, that question was not inappropriate for a young and curious mind and it made one very important point: young people don't really know what Erie was like "when we were kids".

I don't remember exactly how I responded to his question then, but just in case he's been waiting for an answer, allow me to use this space to explain to him after all these years what the city was like when I was a boy.

First of all, Rick, the fact is that many of the streets that we consider part of the city today were really not paved back in the 30's and 40's. For example, I remember traveling up Greengarden Boulevard south of 26th Street and having the pavement end at about 32nd Street. Beyond that point it was just an unpaved dirt road with one rough lane on either side of some wild growth that was eventually to become today's existing boulevard. Speaking of boulevards, there is a boulevard on Liberty Street now that extends from 21st Street up to 26th. I can remember the time when that boulevard extended all the way down to 15th Street. I think it was removed because of the amount of traffic that turned onto Liberty from Brown Avenue on its way to 12th Street and the downtown area.

Much of what is now "Southwest Erie" from Liberty westward to Pittsburgh Avenue and beyond and from 32nd southward to upper Peach Street was just open fields and farm land. My father and my uncle used to have lots in some of those fields up in the vicinity of what is now West 32nd near Raspberry and Elmwood. Lots were parcels of land that city folks rented for a few dollars a year to raise more vegetables than their back yards had room for. Several times a week and every weekend during the summer my dad and his brother would go up and tend their lots, weeding and hoeing around their tomatoes, beans, peppers, zucchini and other vegetables.

The streets west of Ainsworth Field behind Roosevelt School were never paved either and the wooded area just west of 21st and Bauer Lane

44

My father and his brother Egisto working in our garden on West 20th Street where they grew vegetables for our family. They also had a large tract of land up near 32nd and Raspberry where they raised even more vegetables for sale to the various corner grocery stores that were located throughout the west side Italian neighborhoods. Note the grape arbor that was attached to the back of our house. Not only did it produce delicious grapes, but it also served as a great cover over the picnic table and benches that were placed beneath it.

was "the dump", a place where rubbish was left. How exciting it was to travel the paths that wound through that mysterious wild place. To little boys who went there it was an adventure! Sometimes we would even come across places where someone had spent the night. Food cans and discarded bottles littered the ground and the remnants of a campfire were quite evident. Our active imaginations had bandits hiding there during the night. Or maybe they were runaways or just some hoboes who jumped off trains from the nearby 19th Street tracks.

Here are some other interesting facts of days gone by with which you may not be familiar, Rick. Did you know there was once a railroad track that ran along the south side of West 12th Street from about Cranberry Street all the way to Sassafras? The occasional train that ran on those tracks serviced the factories that lined 12th Street and it moved very slowly amidst city traffic. It even stopped for red lights along the way! In a popular newspaper feature of the day called "Ripley's Believe It or Not", it was reported that this was the only train in the United States that stopped for traffic lights. How's that for putting Erie on the map?

Would you also believe there was once a place out at about 25th and Pittsburgh Avenue that was called the "Poor House"? It was the forerunner of the present County home, Pleasant Ridge Manor. I think it had been abandoned by the time I was a boy if I recall correctly, but I remember it as being a big old red brick building that looked like something left over from the Civil War and next to it was its very own small cemetery. To me it was a scary and spooky place. My mother kept reassuring me that although we were not rich, I would never have to live in a Poor House. I hope she was right.

Did you also know there once was a big spread of open fields where Central High School and Sterling Square are now located that was known as the "Circus Grounds"? The big circuses of the time such as Ringling Brothers – Barnum and Baily came there on a regular basis. The whole "big top" thing with elephants, clowns, and side shows was right there at Peach and Cherry Street.

There were other things that were different then too, especially in the downtown area. Would you believe there was a time when all parking downtown was free? It's true, there was a time when you could actually go downtown to shop in the stores that lined State Street and not have to pay a cent to park. You would just find a parking place, pull in, and shop. There were time limits, of course, and these were enforced in a rather unique way. A police officer would patrol the streets and he would put a chalk mark on the front tire of a car parked in a timed zone. If it was a one hour zone, he would return in an hour or so and if he saw a car with a chalk mark he had made, that car would get a parking ticket.

I'll bet you wonder how it could be that parking was free. The answer is that many working class families did not have cars before the war (World War II, that is) so parking spaces were readily available. Most people got to the downtown either by walking (imagine that!) or by bus, so automobile traffic and parking was no big problem.

And the bus service was wonderful. It was inexpensive (a dime, if I recall correctly with transfers costing two cents) and bus routes were numerous with frequent buses running throughout the day. From where I lived in the 900 block of West 20th Street I could take either the Liberty/Elmwood bus from downtown and get off at 20th and Liberty or the West 18th Street bus and get off at one of three possible stops: 18th and Plum, 18th and Cascade or 20th and Raspberry. Getting off at any of those stops was about the same distance to home.

The buses were reliable and busy! Each morning and again at the end of the day when the downtown stores and offices closed (offices at five, stores at five-thirty except on Monday's when they stayed open until nine) busses were packed! Most of the time with standing room only. And get this, on the more popular runs like the West 18th and Pittsburgh Avenue run, buses ran only minutes apart and still each was packed with commuters during the rush hours.

So who were all these people on the buses and where were they going? They were students going to or returning from school and people who worked in the downtown stores and offices. They were people going across town to and from their factory jobs. And, of course, shoppers. But there was another group that we often times forget about in this day and age: people who were going downtown to do their weekly banking.

Yes, Rick, you had to go downtown to do your banking. There was no such thing as a branch bank or ATM's. You went downtown to the State Street banks with your pay envelope (yes, envelope!) with your pay in cash! You would put some in your savings account or Christmas club, pay something on your loan, make a mortgage payment perhaps, and then go around to the various downtown offices to pay your bills. You went to the gas company, the electric company, the telephone company, the water department, and when necessary, to the city tax office. You also went to the stores where you had a charge account or something in layaway and made your payments in cash there too. No Visa Cards. No Master Cards. No Discover or American Express Cards. Our local economy ran strictly on a cash basis.

I remember once in the early 50's when I was working at Perry Square Men's Store hearing a traveling salesman tell about the day that was coming in the near future when we would have one "charge card" to use wherever we went shopping. He said we would use the new cards for everything and we would use them everywhere. Imagine, charging something at the Boston Store with the same card you could use at Trask's or Halle's. Never! Use a charge card at a drug store, at a gas station, in a restaurant? Ridiculous! The general consensus at that time was that such a credit system would never work. Boy, were we wrong!

ᕦᕤ Our first family car, a 1936 Chevy, was purchased in 1942 and was co-owned by my parents and my aunt and uncle. That's my mother behind the wheel and my aunt in the back seat.

Eventually, because of the increased use of cars after World War II, parking did begin to be a problem. You couldn't find parking places near the banks or the offices and if you did find one, you had to put money in a meter. Parking meters? Imagine, no more free parking! If you did have the luck to find a parking space you had to have the right change, a penny or a nickel (yes, Rick, I said "penny" and "nickel" – 12 minutes for one penny, five cents for an hour). Eventually you had to have dimes and then quarters. "Where will it end?" we wondered.

It soon became obvious to everyone that it would be a lot more convenient if we didn't have to go downtown at all to do our banking or to pay our bills. Since the use of checks had begun to be common the bankers decided to put the banks where the people were. They started opening branch banks outside of the center city. Now we could cash our pay checks and even pay our utility bills at a bank nearer to home. Some people began using their new checking accounts to pay their bills by mail.

So going downtown to bank or pay bills became unnecessary and eventually we didn't have to go there for shopping either. The West and East Erie Plazas and the Liberty Plaza and other such small shopping centers began springing up around the inner city. Larger malls also came on the scene with the Central Mall on Peach between 14th and 18th streets in the late 50's, and of course the Millcreek Mall that had begun to be built at the site of the old Kearsarge Airport in the 1960's.

So someday, Rick, Jessica and Michael will ask you what the city was like when you were a boy. You can begin by telling them that you remember when there was no Bayfront Highway, no Bicentennial Tower, no memorial bricks at Dobbins Landing, no library on the bay, no restaurants and stores south of Interchange Road up near the mall. You might even tell them that as a Cub Scout with Troupe #15 at Sacred Heart Church in the mid 60's you remember going on an organized hike to 38th and Pittsburgh Avenue to see where a new highway called "I-79" was being built.

Maybe you will also be able to tell them there used to be a railroad track that ran across the mid section of entire city at 19th Street, just one block away from where your dad grew up.

And you can tell them, too, that most of the streets in Erie (but not all!) were already paved when their grandfather was boy.

• • •

"State Street University": Friends, Fashions, Fun

Much has been written about what the downtown was like in years past: the hustle and bustle, the Boston Store, the convenient shopping. But when I think of the downtown of the '40's and '50's, I think of what a great place it was for high school and college students to work.

My life downtown began one summer day in 1946 shortly after I graduated from the 8th grade at Sacred Heart School. My buddy Armand DiSantis and I decided to dress up and go downtown to look for jobs. It was agreed we would get off the bus at 12th and State, each take one side of the street, and begin going northward store-to-store looking for work. We flipped a coin to see who would work the west side of State Street and who would work the east. I got the east side.

I stood in the doorway of the Union Bank on the main floor of the Commerce Building, wondering where to begin. I didn't think a bank would hire a 14-year-old, so I moved to the Record Bar next door.

No luck. They didn't need any help.

The next stop brought a total surprise. The lady at Mehler's Tailors hired me! A widow with two sons in the service, Mrs. Mehler needed someone to run errands, keep the shop clean, and deliver merchandise to customers. Wow! My first real job! Poor Armand had not been as lucky on the west side of the street.

I traveled to this new job on my bike which I then used to deliver merchandise to customers. I delivered clothing that had either been altered, tailor-made or dry cleaned, and most of my deliveries were to the Brugger Funeral Home on East 9th Street.

I got to be quite good at riding my bike with just one hand, while with the other holding two or three suits on wire hangers in a paper bag slung over my shoulder. Every time I went to Brugger's and other delivery stops, I followed a different route. In no time, I was as familiar with the downtown as I was with my own neighborhood.

I can't remember now how much I earned (25 cents an hour seems to ring a bell) or how many hours a week I worked, but I do remember that for the rest of that summer it was exciting even though I was developing quite a callus on my right shoulder where the suit hangers always rubbed as I rode my bike.

By late summer, I had quit that job and looked forward to beginning high school at Cathedral Prep. Once the school year began, however, I decided to try my luck at finding another job, one that I could go to directly from school. Now that I had some experience, I was much more confident as I continued my job-hunting walk northward on State Street. I began where I had left off, at Mehler's Tailors, going store-to-store and asking, "Do you need help?"

The next successful stop was Conklin's, a department store on the corner of 11th and State. They sold men's and women's clothing, shoes, jewelry and even small appliances and everything was sold on credit! You could buy things there for 50 cents down and 50 cents a week. I was moving up in the world. No more little, old tailor shops for me; I was working in a real downtown store! Unfortunately, the job at Conklin's came to an end when they decided they didn't need a boy any more, so the job seeking walk down State Street continued. Next stop: Richman Brothers at Easter time, 1947.

This was a really great job, I thought. A classy store between 9th and 10th on State with merchandise that was of considerably better quality than anything I had ever seen at Conklin's. I worked the pick-up desk, where I wrapped suits, coats and other merchandise for waiting customers. With the passing of the Easter rush that job, too, came to an end.

My real career downtown was not to begin until the fall of 1947 when a notice on the bulletin board at Prep read: Help wanted – after school and Saturdays. Apply Lloyd's Men's Store, 709 State Street. I couldn't wait for 7th period to end. I ran all the way to the store at the State Street address. I was the first one to get there. Several other guys from school soon followed, but they were too late. I had the job!

What a store! A brand new, very modern, very ritzy haberdashery. What a place to work! This was going to be great. The owners were the Elfenbein brothers. Conrad Elfenbein, an interesting and colorful individual, was the major partner. He and two of his brothers owned three State Street jewelry stores. "Mr. Conrad", as we called him , owned Conrad's Jeweler's at 1001 State in the Baldwin Building. His brother, Marvin, owned Marvin's Jewelers at 703 State, and Philip owned Philip's Jewelers in the 1100 block on the west side of State Street. A fourth brother, Cecil, was local attorney.

This picture was taken in Lloyd's Men's Store which was located at 709 State Street. I worked there all the years I went to Prep and then moved down three doors to Perry Square Clothes at the corner of 7th and State where I worked until I graduated from Gannon College and left for the service in 1954.

This is my cousin Carl behind the wheel of my very first car, a 1946 Chevy. It was green when I first got it in 1951 but eventually had it painted red.

Working for the Elfenbeins, and especially Mr. Conrad, was a great educational experience. He loved Gilbert and Sullivan operettas and often time quoted appropriate lyrics to suit a particular occasions. Not only did he teach me how to properly clean the store but soon he and store manage Ed Dashoffy had me ticketing merchandise, helping to trim the display windows, handling all the packages for the incoming and outgoing mail, and even starting to wait on customers. Eventually, I learned to "cash out" and prepare bank deposits. A great fringe benefit to the job was being able to buy the latest in "cool" clothing at cost. And if a big dance was coming up at school, Mr. Conrad would often let me borrow his car, a huge late-model Chrysler. What a deal! I stayed at Lloyd's for the next four years.

By the end of my first year at Gannon, Lloyd's Men's Store had gone out of business, and I had moved down three doors to work for John Cianella at Perry Square Clothes on the corner of 7th and State. Perry Square was the only place where guys could find the latest in pegged pants, one one-button suits, and other high-style clothing items popular at the time. No Ivy League, preppy-type clothing here. For that you went to the more conservative Bakers' or P.A.Meyers. I had landed in the middle of sartorial splendor.

All of these men's stores were considered to be the really choice spots to work. In fact, they served as a training ground for three of my contemporaries who were to become future store owners themselves: Tom Karle (Tom Karle's Traditional Clothier), Ed Cianella (Park's Men's Wear) and Jack Bataglia (Taggert's).

The best part of working down town was sharing the experience with other high school and college boys. We were the stock boys, the young salesmen or the bank messengers. We dressed well, had a little money in our pockets, and knew everything that was going on downtown. We were a very exclusive club, and many were fellow Prepsters.

Some of those who belonged to this club over the years were: Urbie Volk (Conrad's); Harvey McIvor (Perry Square and First National Bank); Tom and Pat Karle (Baker's Men's Store); John Schwartz (Security Bank); Jim Dehnert and John Heberlien (Lloyd's); Joe DeSanti (Perry Square and Security Bank); Ed Cianella (Perry Square Clothes and Park's Men's Wear); Jack Diebold (Erie Sports Store); Jerry Bova (Perry Square Clothes); and my good friends Carl "Buster" Minzenberger (Boston Store) and Armand DiSantis (Conrad's Jewelers).

The club met regularly for lunch with geography playing an important part in our choice of restaurants. The snack bar in the back of Hall's Cigar Store on the corner of 7th and State was a particular favorite close to where we worked as was Taylor's near 8th and State, the Brown Derby on the corner of 7th and French, and Clark's Restaurant near 10th and State. We rarely ventured to "lower State" which to us meant anything north of Perry Square. There was nothing of interest to us between the park and the public dock. The best place in all of downtown Erie, however, in our estimation, was the "A" Bar, the Alexis between 6th and 7th on State. Everybody who was anybody was there, and Florence, the waitress, was an absolute joy.

There were some restaurants we avoided even though they were convenient to our work places. The LaMeda Tea Room on French Street, for example, was a "ladies' place" with very small portions and just too many blue-haired old matrons for us young guys. The Boston Store Dining Room on the 6th floor was nice, but we never really felt comfortable among the mothers and daughters having lunch there. And the Boston Store cafeteria was also okay, but it was more for shoppers and a place for kids to meet after school. The candy stores, Chacona's and Pulakos', served light lunch fare, but our manly appetites drove us elsewhere.

The five-and-dimes, Kresge's, Woolworth's, and Murphy's had lunch counters, but no self respecting sharpie in peg pants would want to be seen there. The "A" Bar, yes. A five-and-dime, never.

It was a great life. We were in the middle of everything that was going on, most of it legal. We knew all the politicians, the cops on the beat, and the Damon Runyon characters who frequented the same hangouts as we did. We met them in the restaurants, the newsrooms and the barber shops.

At two infamous "newsrooms", Larson and Kaminski's just off State Street on W. 7th, and Devlin's on State between 6th and 7th, we could buy our papers, cigarettes, soft drinks and snacks and find the posted ball scores among other things.

And there were the wonderful barber shops. These, too, were places where you met the "movers and shakers" and picked up the latest in State Street gossip. The shop on the second floor over Hall's was a popular one that had to be entered by climbing an open iron stairway on 7th Street. On 9th Street another outside stairway took you to the basement of the Marine Bank to a landmark barber shop with floors and walls done completely in black and white ceramic tile.

Rudy Bauer's Shop on 8th between State and Peach with four (or was it five?) barbers on duty at all times was another busy spot, especially on Gannon's ROTC inspection day. The classiest shop of all, however, was Sam and Ralph's on the corner of 8th and French. They worked only by appointment (unheard of in those days) and you could get a manicure there as well as a shave and a haircut.

The downtown had everything.

Now years later, I look back on those days and remember them fondly. Not only did I have a great wardrobe and an interesting circle of friends, but I also earned enough to buy and maintain a 1946 red Chevy convertible, and pay my $10 per credit college tuition. And all of this while learning a lot about business, about people and about life. I also came to appreciate The Pirates of Penzance.

Over the years, whenever I filled out a job application and came to the part on "education", I was always tempted to write: "Graduated from Cathedral Prep, Gannon College, and State Street University."

• • •

NUNS:
"BLACK BEARS DON'T GO TO HEAVEN"

When I look back at my formative years in Catholic schools my most vivid memories are of the nuns who taught us. They were a most interesting group of women, each with her own personality, her own special "quirks", and many with nick-names ("Bloody Mary") that were for us students the world's most carefully guarded secrets – we thought.

I entered Sacred Heart School's first grade in 1938 and began 12 years of instruction from some absolutely outstanding teachers. The first nun I ever met was Sr. Bonitta, a Sister of St. Joseph. I really don't remember too much about that first year in school but I do remember a small framed holy picture of St. Joseph Sister gave me as a reward for perfect attendance. Now almost sixty years later I still have that picture.

Sr. Benita and I met again some years later when she was working for Catholic Charities. She came to interview me and my wife for background information on a couple who were applying to adopt a baby through Sister's office. She was exactly as I remembered her, short, cheerful, and with a most pleasing smile. Of the two of us, it seemed that I was the only one who had aged. That experience of meeting nuns who had been former teachers was to happen many times over the years and each time I was amazed at how young and active they still were. Back in school we just thought all nuns were old. To find out years later that they were still alive and active just added to their mystique.

At Sacred Heart I encountered a whole string of nuns that were quite memorable. Sr. Euphrasia was my second grade teacher. I had Sr. Benigna in third grade and Sr. Roseann in fourth. In fifth grade it was Sr. Wilma and in sixth Sr. Andrea.

Sr. Andrea was one of the first nuns in the city to work in the black community and her interest in this minority had a definite impact on all of us in her class. She brought African-Americans into our classroom as guests and even provided opportunities for us to work on projects with her at the then recently established church of the Immaculate Conception on Erie's east side. For most of us this was our first contact ever with people of a different race and she taught us lessons of acceptance and tolerance that would serve us well in later years.

In seventh grade there were Sr. Virginia Ann and Sr. Marie Agnes. I remember Sr. Virginia Ann as being the most beautiful lady I ever saw. It wasn't until years later when nuns began using their family names again that I learned her last name was Gardner and that she was the sister of Erie's former mayor, Art Gardner.

About two years ago my family had occasion to attend a Mass at the Sisters of St. Joseph Motherhouse where Sr. Virginia now lives. When I introduced Sister to my granddaughter, Jessica expressed surprise that Sister even remembered who I was after all these years. Sister's response to that was quite a shock: "Oh, I remember him well, Jessica. He sat in the last seat of the second row."

Sr. Marie Agnes' class was interesting because it was a split grade with half the room being 8th graders and the other half being 7th. In an attempt to teach us some social skills, Sister occasionally allowed us to bring in records to play them in class and sometimes she even allowed us to dance! Wow, was she ever progressive!

Our principal in the early years was Sr. Charlotte and by eighth grade her place was taken by Sr. Virginella. What I remember most about Sr. Virginella was how proud she was of her family, the Chisholm family of Erie. She often spoke of them and her experiences as a child. She was gentle and kind, yet an effective disciplinarian. She was a good principal and she prepared us well for the high school years that were to come.

Cathedral Prep in the late 40's also had a wonderful group of nuns, many of whom became legends in their own time. Sisters Mary Elaine, Cherubim (or was it Seraphim?) and Ellen Frances were Sisters of St. Joseph from the Villa. Sisters of Mercy included Imelda, Gertrude, DePaul, Loretta and the legendary "Tessie May" (a.k.a. Sr. Theresa Marie).

To say that Tessie Mae and her "buddy", Sr. Imelda, were colorful would be putting it mildly. They were probably the most popular nuns on the faculty. Sr. Imelda was short, dynamic, and often times quite funny. With Tessie May, on the other hand, you started a relationship in absolute terror after all the horror stories you heard from former students of hers and just hoped for the best. She was a demanding task master who taught Algebra and Latin and in her classes you learned – "or else". When your year in Tessie Mae's class ended, however, you knew you had accomplished something. Not only had you learned a lot but you had survived. Now you too had stories to add to the legend.

🎵 This picture was taken in 1981 at the 35th Reunion of the Sacred Heart Class of 1946 and it includes some of the teachers we had in grade school.

- First row: Sr. Hidergarde (a member of our class), Sr. Wilma, Sr. Andrea, Sr. Benita (my 1st grade teacher), Sr. Virginella, Sr. Mary James, Sr. Lucy, and classmate Dot Zupanik.
- Second row: Joan Wolf Stolz (not visible), Katie Tucker Considine, Joyce McFadden Mueck, Barb Lindsey Rodgers, Dorothy Brie Marsh, Antionette Berarducci Mucci, Jean Weschler, Jean Walker Ring, Rose Triana Seip, and Audrey Schlindwein Mascharka.
- Third Row: Jack Haller, Dave Flanagan, Henry Kanyar, Bill Beyer, & Norman Grode.
- Fourth Row: Jim Timon, Ed and Dick Koscelnik, Jim MacKrell, Bill Detter, Dick Karle, Tom Karle, Joe Pettinato, Gilbert Berchtold, Joe Lazar.

I did not attend this reunion because of the death of my father two days earlier.

In August of 2001 we will be celebrating our 55th reunion of our 8th grade class.

Actually, Tessie May's bark was much worse than her bite and the reputation that preceded her made her much more frightening than was necessary. She was, in fact, an excellent teacher who absolutely knew how to talk to and work with boys. She came from a family of seven brothers and, as she often said, if she could survive growing up in that household dealing with mere Prepsters was a piece of cake. She talked tough, she walked tough, she was tough. You always knew what was expected of you and you knew darn well you couldn't get away with a thing. Each year the legend grew and spreading stories to wide eyed freshman of the infamous "Tessie Mae" became part of the initiation to Prep.

I remember one incident that showed a side of Tessie May that many of us had never seen before. It happened toward the end of the school day some time in late May in my freshman year in 1947. As we sat very quietly working in Sister's 7th period Algebra class we could hear a lot of noise out in the halls as the graduating seniors were celebrating their final day in school. Suddenly our classroom door began to open and very slowly a good size black bear cub entered the room. Everybody gasped. Immediately we all turned towards Sister. This was going to be exciting. Somebody was going to be in big trouble here. Heads would roll.

Sister turned and glared at the bear as only she could glare and then a slight smile lit up her face. She began to giggle, then laugh. She tried desperately to conceal her laughter but there was nothing she could do to hide it. She was thoroughly enjoying this delightful intrusion. It was a stuffed bear on wheels! The seniors had just come to say good-bye to one of their favorite teachers.

The Benedictine Sisters who taught at Prep also had reputations that preceded them. Sr. Adalaide was a brilliant math teacher who taught well into her advanced years, even after her hearing was almost totally gone, but she stayed on because she loved "her boys". She often had us pray for those Prepsters who had died in World War II and whose names were listed on the plaque on the base of the statue of the Virgin Mary, Our Lady of Prep, that is located on the school campus. Sister had known and taught all of them and praying for them was her way of honoring their memory.

Sr. Virginia, OSB, (English and Spanish) was small but fearless and an excellent teacher. About 20 years after graduating I chaperoned a group of Millcreek students to a regional student council convention at Kennedy Christian High School in Oil City and lo and behold who did I see but Sr. Virginia. She had aged a little but she really hadn't changed at all, still lively and vivacious and interested in everything. It was the first time I had seen her in her order's more modern garb and she looked wonderful.

Sr. Pat (Patricia), another from St. Ben's, made everybody in her classes wear a tie even before Prep had adopted an official dress code. In fact, it was her insistence on ties that eventually led to the rule being applied to the whole school. From there to mandatory sweaters and blazers was just a short move. And as they say, "the rest is history."

Benedictine Sr. Alexia taught typing. On the first day of school sister always went around the room to tell each new student which upperclassman had sat at that very typewriter the year before and what a wonderful typist he had become. But a classroom full of boys learning to type certainly seemed silly at the time. It was especially silly the day we had to type to music: "Listen to the rhythm boys. Move your fingers to the rhythm". It was really hard to take this class seriously, but I am grateful today that she had the strength to persevere. It was the most useful class I have ever had and the skills I learned there I have used on an almost daily basis through college, the military and in my working life. Sister would be pleased to see how many of us our using those skills today not with our typewriters but with our computers.

In time many of these religious women changed their mission within their respective communities. They went from being primarily teachers to workers in various other fields: they went into professional careers; became administrators of programs in hospitals and nursing homes; and became parish leaders or religious education specialists. They went out and worked in the "real world" serving our community in new and different ways. Sr. Andrea, for example, went from teaching to founding the St. Martin Center in Erie's African-American community. Times were changing and the nuns of the Erie Diocese were changing with them.

Which brings me to the point of this Flashback. So often in life we come to realize that we may have missed an opportunity to say thank you to people who made a difference in our lives. Hoping that is not the case today, let me now officially express my gratitude to all the nuns who in some way touched my life or the lives of members of my family.

To the teachers, the nurses, the care givers I say thank you for being there. Thank you for setting such good examples for all of us to follow and thank you for caring. Thank you too for your prayers and your support in times of trouble and sorrow. But most of all, thank you for giving your lives in service to others and helping to make us the men and women we are today.

And to Tessie Mae, I say, "Rest in peace, Sister, and fear not. Black bears don't go to heaven."

• • •

"We'll Always Be Loyal and True": My High School Reunion

Well, it has finally happened. I've begun to feel old.

It is not because of the graying hair or the aches and pains I now experience with increasing frequency. It is not even because I am no longer able to do many of the things I did before. What has put me over the edge is a letter I received recently from Paul Kraus, a high school classmate, announcing that our 50th year class reunion would be held in September of 2000.

Fifty years!! Impossible. It seems it was only yesterday that we graduated from Cathedral Prep in our white dinner jackets and black ties on the ninth street lawn of the school campus. It can't be a half a century since I marched across the field at the stadium as drum major of the band. It can't be that long ago that we went to dances in the gym, hung out at Block's Pool Room, ate after-school snacks in the Boston Store cafeteria, and cheered our teams on to victory. It just can't be fifty years ago!

Or can it?

Now that I think about it, I guess it has been a long time. As I look around I see that things have changed. For one thing I don't think kids get to school the same way we used to. We used a mode of transportation that is almost unheard of today: we walked! My buddies Armand DiSantis, Carl "Buster" Minzenberger, Norman Grode and I used to meet at 21st and Liberty every morning and begin our trek down Liberty Street and over 10th to Prep (Norman went to Tech) and we were not alone. Other neighborhood kids going to the Villa, the old Tech School, and Strong Vincent were also going north on the "Liberty Express Way". Nuns from the Villa Maria convent were walking south at that same time on their way to Sacred Heart and St. Michael's schools for the day's classes.

The return trip home was somewhat different. Many of us had jobs downtown immediately after school so we went home by bus later in the day. I worked at Lloyd's Men's Store, Buster worked at the Boston Store and Armand worked at Conrad's Jewelers.

Another change I see is in the downtown itself. It was a very busy place after school fifty years ago. There were the Pulokos' and Chacona's candy stores with soda bars for a quick coke or ice cream soda; the lunch counters in the "Five and Dimes" such as Murphy's and Kresgee's and, of course, the ever popular Boston Store Cafeteria in the store's basement. There was even a special entrance to the cafeteria down a narrow stairway which was entered from an almost unnoticeable doorway on the 8th street side of the store. After school Prep traffic was also heavy on its way to Block's Pool Room (no girls allowed!) in the 700 block of State upstairs of Taylor's Bar.

The intersections at 8th, 9th and 10th and State were big bus transfer points for kids on their way home from school. In addition to kids from public schools, girls from St. Ben's and the Villa would be there to transfer to the four corners of the city. And the Prep boys would be there checking out the field.

It was during these times in the late 40's and early 50's that Prep reached a turning point it its history. The new school building adjacent to the Cathedral had just been completed in 1944 and the school was experiencing a growth in enrollment. It was then, too, that we began to become a power house in local athletics. Unfortunately, I was not one who contributed to that athletic prominence. I played in the band.

Coach Walt Strosser did ask me once to go out for track. "With those long legs you'd be great for the hurdles", he said. But I had an after-school job and, besides, physical activity was not one of my major interests. So I settled for being in the band from which many of my fondest memories of my Prep days originated.

꙾ This is a picture of the Prep band marching in a State Street parade with me as the drum major. With that white fur hat I was over 7.5 feet tall.

61

The 10th year reunion of the Prep Class of 1950.

- First row on the floor from left: Don Guerrein, Joe Berdis, Bob Davies, Larry Simmons, Gino Carlotti, Jim Condon, and Tom Karle.
- Kneeling behind the first row: Frank Kleinhanz, Tom Kearney, Bill Beyer, Bill Deluca.
- Seated: Art Dietz, Chuck Dietz, Fred DeLuca, Armand DeSantis, Fr. Daniel Martin, Nick Konzel, Dan Ropelewski, John Stolz, Mike Carey, Ralph "Midge" Causgrove.

- First row standing: Joe Wilczynski, Chuck "Skip" McCallion, Bob Hagerty, Tom Ward, Leo Kleinhanz, Paul Burke, Dick Leary, Ed Heubel, Ray McQuillan, Jim Bougie, Tony Lackovic, Tom McGraw, Jim Dehnert, Bob Bujalski, Chet Prylinski.
- Second row standing: Joe Hoyt, Jim MacKrell, Dick Rahner, Jack Dill, Don Welsh, Dan Meahl, John Rumpf, Dick Gerbracht, Jack Crotty, Ed Wilwohl, Bob Held.
- Top row: Jerry Jerge, Jack Haller, Richard Gardner, Edgar Smith, Jim Kaveny, Jim Scully, Dick Zimmer, Emil "Bill" Detter, Jack Dalton, Chuck Haller.

The first three years I played a trumpet. Although I was no great musician, it was an interesting experience and I came to know some very interesting guys: Bill Buseck, Lou Cavanaugh, Bill and Chuck Graves, Frank Kuntz, Joe Hoyt, Jim Dehnert to name a few and William "Butterball" Karg who was to go on and become a priest of the Erie Diocese. Charlie Conti, an old neighborhood buddy, played the glockenspeil. He too is now a priest, "Fr. Cornelius Gerard" of the Franciscans stationed in St. Petersburg, Florida.

I might add here that none of my fellow band members ever made it to the Julliard School of Music that I know of. We were not the greatest band in the world, let me tell you, but we tried. Band practice was fun and being involved in all the football games, road trips, parades, rallies, and other activities made it really a rewarding activity.

As a marching band we didn't look too great either. For the first football game in the stadium when I was a freshman in the fall of 1946 we didn't even have uniforms. They had been ordered at the end of the previous school year but did not arrive in time for the first game so in our usual "do or die" spirit we marched into the stadium wearing black pants, white shirts with black ties, and Prep sweaters. The sweaters were black cardigans with orange trim. "Real dorks", as my grandchildren would say today.

But the uniforms did finally arrive before the second or third game of the season and from that point on we marched in style behind our leader, Jim Runser. The following year the drum major was Jim MacNamara. That's right, we were "MacNamara's Band"!!

When our football team actually began winning games in city series competition, a somewhat new experience for Prep, the band began a short lived tradition about which most people may have forgotten. After almost every game we won in the stadium during the football season of 1949 the band would not go back to school on the bus. Instead, we would form up and march down State Street with throngs of kids following behind. We became an unofficial one band parade with no parade permit and no police escort. Talk about traffic congestion!

When Jim McNamara graduated in 1949 I was drafted to replace him as drum major. I wish I could say I was selected because of my talent as a musician, but that was not the case. I wasn't picked because of my leadership abilities either. There was just one reason I was to become the third drum major in Prep's history: I fit the uniform. At that time I was 6'4" and weighed 150 pounds and the uniform was made for

64

a tall skinny kid. And what a uniform it was! All white with brass buttons and braid all over the thing. The crowning touch was the hat, about eighteen inches of white fur! With the hat on I was over seven feet tall. What a sight!

That tall hat came in handy too. It was a wonderful place to store stuff as we marched down the middle of the field: a plastic raincoat, gloves, newspaper to sit on so as to keep the white pants clean, and candy bars. Candy bars and other snacks were important "equipment". Although I was thin as a rail I ate like most growing teenagers – constantly! The only problem with storing all these supplies in the hat was that with the extra weight, trying to keep everything under control on a windy football field was quite a task. I was top heavy but it was worth the effort.

Which reminds me of the Prep cafeteria where I always found the food to be good and plentiful. In fact, I bought the full lunch everyday plus "doubles" if it was something I really liked and I always had two hot dogs on the side. The cafeteria ladies used to feel sorry for me because I spent so much for lunch so to help me out they would often place the "double" (a slice of meat loaf, a piece of chicken or an extra pork chop) under the double scoop of mashed potatoes so the cashier couldn't see what was there and I wouldn't have to pay for the extras. Nice ladies.

I also remember lunch time very well not only for the food but for the time we had after lunch to go out and grab a smoke. Yes, young people, we actually had smoking areas where we were allowed to smoke. Well, maybe "allowed" is too strong a term. Let's say there were places where we could get away with it. One place was between the stairways leading up to the entrance to St. Peter's Cathedral. Eventually somebody became concerned with all the cigarette butts that littered the walkway on Sassafras, so we were "allowed" to move to the bike racks next to the entrance to Prep's Athletic Department on 10th Street.

On any day we were to play Tech, our rival school across the street, the 10th and Sassafras corner became the scene of "instant pep rallies". Guys from our cafeteria would gather on the northwest corner and get into a cheering match with the Tech guys on their southeast corner. I don't recall those occasions ever getting out of hand. Well, maybe an apple would be lobbed from one corner to the other but that was about as rough as it got. They were just good natured enthusiastic events that ended without incident when the lunch period was over. And at the end of the season one of these two schools would be awarded the "Little

Brown Jug", the trophy for winning the game between these two friendly competitors.

When our Class of 1950 meets in September I'm sure we will be
swapping stories such as these about the good times we had at Prep.
We'll remember the nuns, the priests, the coaches, and we'll remember
the characters in our classes and the crazy things we did. We'll turn the
clocks back to a time when we were boys. Maybe, just maybe, there will
be somebody there whose hair is grayer than mine. There may even be
somebody who has gained more weight than I. And there certainly will
be those whose absence will be sadly noted for the list of deceased members grows with every reunion.

But for that one night we won't be old men anymore. We'll all be
boys again, Prepsters, fondly remembering the days of our youth. I just
hope we have a good turnout. After all, it isn't everyday you have a 50th
reunion. It should be fun.

● ● ●

GANNON COLLEGE:
OUR WINDOW ON THE WORLD

A few weeks ago I received an unexpected phone call from Wiley Jinks, an old army buddy I first met at R.O.T.C. summer camp in 1952 when I was a sophomore at Gannon College. After graduating and being commissioned 2nd lieutenants, Wiley and I met again on active duty during 16 weeks of Officers' Basic Training at Camp Gordon, Georgia before Wiley shipped out for Europe and before I went to Korea. For over forty years we never saw nor heard from each other again until his recent phone call from Hugo, Oklahoma. That call prompted me to dig out some old photo albums to look for pictures of Wiley and our days at Camp Gordon. In doing so I came across a packet of pictures from Gannon in the years from 1950 to 1954. As I looked at the familiar faces in those photos I began to remember those college days and to think about how different things are today.

In the fall of 1950 Gannon was not yet a university. It was a small private all male liberal arts college that enrolled mostly young men from the greater Erie area. The 80 graduates in the class of 1954 were a mix of recent high school graduates and returning World War II veterans who were just beginning their delayed education through the G.I. Bill of Rights. Although all of us were full-time students, most also had full or part-time jobs around town. Holding jobs was easy because the college scheduled most classes in the morning with only science labs in the afternoon. For the "vets", of course, these jobs were a necessity for most were married and had young families. For us younger students the work provided the funds we needed to pay for our schooling.

And pay we did. Ten dollars a credit! That's what the fees were when I was a freshman but after a year or two they went up to $13 per credit. Imagine, a 33% increase! Because there was very little financial aid in those days, the college agreed that a "no increase" policy would be instituted for students who were already enrolled. If you started as a freshman at $10 you remained at $10. The $13 fee only applied to new incoming students. Fair enough, but even at those prices most of us had to take out loans to pay our tuition and other fees.

The registration process at the beginning of each semester involved a trip to the treasurer's office where we sat down with an upcoming young banker, Mike Veshecco of the Bank of Erie, to work out the loan details. Many years later Mike retired as the President of Penn Bank and shortly after that my wife and I moved from our home in the city out to Millcreek, three doors away from Mike and Betty Veshecco.

What I remember most about my college days was being in the R.O.T.C. With our country involved in the Korean War, it was mandatory for all freshmen and sophomores to be in R.O.T.C. unless, of course, one could not pass the entrance physical or had already served in the military. As an incentive for students to remain in the program beyond the required first two years, the government paid juniors and seniors a monthly allotment of $27. Strangely enough, that amount was exactly equal to my monthly loan payment at the bank. Because we knew we would be drafted as soon as we graduated, many of us did in fact elect to stay in the program for the full four years. We did so not so much for the money, although that certainly was an incentive, but because we figured if military service was inevitable it would be better to go into the service as an officer rather than as an enlisted man.

Some of the "vets" joined R.O.T.C. with the intent of reentering the service to launch a second career as an army officer. One old friend who planned on such a move was a former army sergeant by the name of Luther Manus. To say that "Luke" was an interesting member of the student body would be an understatement. He was married, had a family, had served in the military, and was the first Afro-American I ever met who could speak Italian. The war stories he told only added to his legend. After graduation he returned to the military as a commissioned officer, retired after a few years and came back home to become a teacher and counselor in the Erie City schools. Now retired from that second

The Gannon College ROTC Battalion at a formal review in 1953 at Bay View Field. I was the drum major for this, Gannon's first and only Drum and Bugle Corps.

career he owns the AM Convenience store at 12th and French.

The R.O.T.C. program consisted of several components. There was the classroom instruction which took place in a converted private residence on the southwest corner of Sixth and Sassafras and the weekly drill day when all cadets had to be in uniform, pass inspection, and go to afternoon drill sessions. In the winter months the drills were held in the Gannon Auditorium (now the Hammermill Center). In better weather we marched to Bayview Field at 2nd and Cherry.

By my junior year the corps had grown to the point that we were able to field a drum and bugle corps so that we could march to Bayview in style with a drum beat to keep the cadence. At least once each year, usually in the spring, the corps of cadets carried out a full-scale formal battalion review parade, music and all, for an audience of school officials, Bishop John Mark Gannon, Bayview neighbors, and parents. I was the drum major.

A third component was the social life. There were various R.O.T.C. functions throughout the year but the highlight of the College's social calendar was the annual Military Ball. This was a formal affair that was held in the auditorium with all the pomp and circumstance the military could muster. It was here each year that one cadet's date would be named "Co-Ed Cadet Colonel" with a visiting dignitary pinning the Silver Eagles on the shoulders of the young lady's just-for-the-evening uniform. My buddy Roy Bliley's girlfriend, Pearl Tallow, was the "Colonel" in our senior year.

The most challenging part of R.O.T.C. training was the six week summer camp at the Provost Marshall's Military Police school at Camp Gordon, Georgia. For me, going to that camp in the summer of 1952 was the first time ever I was away from home for more than two nights. It was also the first time I rode on a train, the first time I was south of the

Mason-Dixon Line, and the first time I lived in close quarters with guys from all parts of the country. My fellow cadets were from Alabama, California, Louisiana, New Jersey, Ohio, South Carolina and Texas. Among my friends from Gannon who joined me for this "learning experience" were, Joe Salvia, Joe Archer, Jim Niland, Walter Nagorski, and the legendary "Luke" Manus, to name a few.

Usually cadets attended this camp in the summer between their junior and senior years, but in the early 1950's because of the military buildup during the Korean conflict, colleges instituted a mandatory "accelerated program" for cadets requiring them to go to school for two full summers and in so doing, complete their college work in 3-1/2 years. They would thus be able to go on active duty sooner so as to fill the ever increasing need for young officers. I went to school during the summers of 1951 and 1953 and to R.O.T.C. camp in the summer of 1952. I went on active duty as a 2nd Lieutenant in U.S. Army Military Police Corps in February of 1954. In the Gannon College commencement program for the graduation ceremonies of May of '54, my buddies and I who were already on active duty were simply listed as "in absentia"

My memories of Gannon, however, are not restricted to R.O.T.C. I remember well the college's physical plant which was not the sprawling campus that exists today. Most classes were held in Old Main where the beautiful hardwood parquet floors were not yet covered over by tile or the carpeting that came in years later. The spacious bedrooms and sitting rooms on the second floor of the Strong mansion were our classrooms and each varied in decor with its distinctive plaster moldings, uniquely carved fireplaces and ornately framed mirrors over the mantels. The beautiful louvered shutters that folded up into the walls were still in wonderful working condition. The rooms on the third floor where some administrative offices were located and where some classes were held were somewhat smaller and less elegant. Obviously these were servants quarters in the days of Annie Strong.

ROTC Advance Corps of junior and senior officers for the 1953-54 school year.

- First Row: Frank Stanovich, Richard Burkholder, Leaonard Lechner, Joseph Salvia, Donald Becker, Gino Carlotti, James Beveridge, Walter Nagorski, Charles Foshay, Royal Bliley
- Second Row: unknown, Thomas Malloy, Angelo Pivetta, L. Kaczenski, unknown, William Reuscher, Ray Ward, Paul Kraus, Norbert Walczak, Robert Lorigan.
- Third Row: J. Proctor, unknown, K. Schmitt, James Niland, Edward Hejnowski, J. Singer, J. Barczyk, Richard Zaworski, Ray Francis.

Several classes were held in the far west wing of Old Main on the first floor level of what was then the new library, and science labs were held in the carriage house behind Old Main. In the basements under the library and Old Main was the commons area and the cafeteria. The cafeteria was really a short order grill that featured only fountain items, hot dogs and hamburgers, and one or two daily specials, but it was the perfect place to grab a quick bite between classes or before rushing off to work. It was at those tables down in the basement that Bill DeLuca taught me how to play pinochle.

I also fondly remember the outstanding faculty.

Because the college was small, class sizes were such that one came to know professors on a very personal level. A number of them had come from the illustrious academic centers of Europe as refugees at the end of the war. Father Alphonse Crispo from Italy never failed to begin his philosophy class lectures exactly where he had ended on the previous session, and he did so without the use of notes. Father Bonaventure Ciufoli, from a prominent family of Roman nobility, taught Philosophy, Ethics, Marriage Guidance, Art Appreciation and Italian and he did so in an interesting and colorful way that made his classes very popular. His hobby was music and students often spent their leisure hours in his quarters listening to Italian operas from Father's extensive record collection. Father Joseph Barr from Lithuania taught Political Science and was the founder of Gannon's well known Model United Nations that is still providing an important learning experiences for local high school students who participate in the program each year.

Other teachers who contributed to the cosmopolitan atmosphere of Gannon's early years were: Father Domokos (from Yugoslavia, I believe,) who later changed his name to Finn and is now a frequent contributor of columns in the Erie papers; French Canadian philosopher Father Gougoux; Sociologist Dr. Helen Zand from a scholarly Polish background; and the Hungarian portrait artist Zoltan Heya. Mr. Heya's wife operated the book store and his daughter assisted in the library.

With so many foreign teachers and staff members around we used to joke that at the end of our four years of study we would be lucky if we emerged from college without accents. Fortunately, we had some great "English speaking" teachers, too. "Doc" Beyer (Beyer Hall) was probably the best History teacher I ever had. And I will never forget Fathers Franz, Shanz, Levis, Peterson and Russell (Russell Hall). They were good priests and scholarly teachers who guided us through a demanding curriculum, one that required every student to minor in Philosophy. Father Wilfred Nash (Nash Library), who was Dean of the college in the early fifties, knew almost the entire student body by name. Years after he retired he still never failed to greet old Gannon grads whenever he met them.

Some former faculty members went on to rather successful careers in other fields. Athletic Director and football coach Lou Tullio became Mayor of Erie, as did Business Administration teacher Art Gardner. Science teacher Dr. Joseph Zipper became Superintendent of the Erie Public Schools.

 Me at my desk in Munsanee, Korea, in 1955 where I served as Aide de Camp to Major General Harlan C. Parks, senior officer of the United Nations Armistice Commission.

Yes, my memories of Gannon are of a friendly, comfortable place where one could get a good education at minimal cost without having to leave home. It was a school that had wonderful teachers and an interesting student body, and for us young Erie boys it became our window on the world.

I'm glad Wiley Jinks called to rekindle these fond memories.

• • •

LONDON'S ST. PAUL'S CATHEDRAL AND THE ERIE CONNECTION

St. Paul's Cathedral in London, England.
Photo courtesy of St. Paul's Cathedral.

One Sunday morning Mrs. Millie Borsa, a member of our parish, stopped me after church to tell me she had a book she thought I might like to have. Her son had bought it at a house sale years ago and she was getting rid of some old things she had found in the attic and was about to throw it out. But she hated to do so, she said, because the book seemed somewhat special and since I was interested in history perhaps I would like to have it. In a matter of minutes she went home and returned with book in hand.

That evening I sat down to see what unknown treasures this faded blue cloth-bound relic might hold. What I found was a remarkable short book about some little known events related to World War II. And tucked into its back pages was a 1953 letter to an Erie family from *The Times of London*. Could that letter be an "Erie Connection" to the events described in the book itself?

This Flashback is the story – the unfinished story – of that book and the letter it contained.

Entitled *Britain's Homage to 28,000 American Dead*, the book is only sixty-seven pages long and was published in 1952 by *The Times of London*. The preface opens with these lines:

> Only time heals the scars of war, but those who survive take renewed pride from the commemoration of the dead. This book tells the story of the creation of a British memorial to the Americans who lived and died in Britain's midst in the Second World War.

Following a short message from Prime Minister Winston Churchill, Chapter One tells of the events begun in 1939 that would bring many thousands of American service men and women to the British Isles over the next five or six years. The story of how these Americans adjusted to this foreign land and its people (and they to the Americans) is interesting and often times humorous. It reminded me of the complaint of the British about American military personnel that was often quoted in the United States during and after the war: "The problem with the Americans is that they are over paid, over sexed, and over here!" But in fact, the book's description of how these two nations of "cousins" actually came to live, work, and fight together reveals a high degree of mutual admiration and respect.

What was especially poignant for the British people was that 28,000 of the Americans who had been stationed at British bases lost their lives during the war. They were killed either in Britain itself or while on active service in other war zones after having been stationed on British soil. The closing lines of the first chapter state that "Cambridge, the university town, now holds the largest United States military cemetery in Britain. Scores of other places in Britain are, in a special sense, dedicated to the memory of men from a not so foreign country who died so that others might continue the pursuit of life, liberty and happiness."

But the real story, the one that most Americans today know nothing about, begins in Chapter Three on page 37. Here in great detail is outlined the birth of an idea to honor the memory of the 28,000 British-based Americans who lost their lives in World War II. The implementation of that idea began with an appeal published in British newspapers in November of 1945, six months after VE Day. It was in the form of a letter over the signatures of Marshal of the Royal Air Force Lord Trenchard and Sir Clive Baillieu, President and Chairman respectively of the American and British Commonwealth Association. The letter called for the creation of an American Chapel in Sir Christopher Wren's famous London cathedral, St. Paul's.

Although heavily damaged during the bombings of London, St. Paul's still stood as the "Metropolitan Cathedral of the Empire and as the symbol of the faith and endurance of the British people." It was suggested that at the east end of this magnificent church, in the semi-circular apse behind the main altar where once stood the bombed out Jesus Chapel, an American Chapel should be constructed. The proposal was put before the Chapter of the Cathedral and was sincerely welcomed with this response:

> No nobler, nor more sanctified ground for an American Chapel in London could have been found than a place in St. Paul's, in the heart of the City. The national cathedral and the parish church of the British ommonwealth, St. Paul's enshrines not a little of the history of British valor and sacrifice. Within its walls lie or are commemorated a host of the greatest of Britain's fighting leaders, Nelson and Wellington among them. The American comrades-at-arms of the British people thus commemorated in St. Paul's would keep noble company.

As the idea of this memorial to Americans grew it gained the support of His Majesty King George who even granted permission for the use of his name when an appeal for funds was published. General Eisenhower, also in favor of the plan, proposed that the Americans contribute the actual Roll of Honour of the American dead that was to be enshrined in the chapel. "This", he pointed out, "could only be the task of American hands."

The published letter proposing the idea called for the people of Britain to build this memorial – not any official governmental body –

and they could do so by contributing their "pennies, their sixpences, or their pounds, as the case may be". The appeal went on to inform the public that contributions could be paid over the counter of any bank in the British Isles, and that the names of subscribers would not be published. Thus, under the supervision of a council to be set up under the chairmanship of the Archbishop of Canterbury, the chapel would be built by anonymous contributions.

In all, several million people in the British Isles contributed a total of nearly £100,000. The contributions, received at 664 branch banks in Britain, came in the form of cash, checks, postal money orders, and stamps. Approximately 4,000 of these contributions were accompanied by letters from all parts of the country. The book recounts that the contributions came from "the eminent and the obscure, from village groups and parochial church councils and golf clubs, from grown-ups and children, from people in ones or twos who preferred to remain anonymous." The letters were written on every kind of writing paper, from "the heavily embossed kind to a sheet from a child's exercise book." One such note was the following:

> It is a very small sum I have enclosed for such a great purpose, but I know it will be received with courtesy. I felt I would like to contribute to the memory of those dear boys. We had so many staying close to us and they came as members of our family to our fireside, so will we always remember them with gratitude and deep affection.

Work on the chapel did not begin until February of 1951. The work of national reconstruction of war damaged homes, industry and communications took priority over the building of this memorial to the Americans. It was estimated that it would take three or possibly four more years to complete the project.

The Roll of Honour, however, was completed early that year. Designed and executed in the United States, it consisted of 473 pages listing the names of the 28,000 American men and women of all branches of the service who were to be memorialized in the chapel. It was decided that the presentation of that roll should be made to St. Paul's as soon as possible. The date selected for this special ceremony, a date that had significance both for the people of Britain and of the United States, was July Fourth of 1951.

During the bombing of London in World War II, the famous St. Paul's Cathedral lost its "Christ Chapel" which was later rebuilt and renamed the "American Chapel". It is in that chapel that now rests the "Roll of Honour" containing the names of the 28,000 Americans who died during that war after having been stationed on British soil.

Photo courtesy of St. Paul's Cathedral.

The book describes, in very great detail, the pomp and ceremony with which the red leather bound volume with its gold-tooled front cover was presented by General Eisenhower to the Dean of the Cathedral. There is the order of procession, the hymns that were sung, the scripture readings, and excerpts of the prayers that were said and the homilies that were preached. There is also a listing of the many dignitaries in attendance. The royal family was represented by the Queen, Princess Elizabeth, and Princess Margaret. The King, although fully in support of the project, could not attend due to illness. And it is there in St. Paul's Cathedral that now rests the Roll of Honour as an integral part of the sanctuary.

The American Chapel was finally completed in 1955, two years after Britain's Homage to 28,000 American Dead was published. The closing paragraph of the book's preface states that a copy of the book was being presented "to the next-of-kin of each of the 28,000 Americans whose sacrifice is therein commemorated."

Tucked in between the last page and the cover of the book that Millie Borsa gave me was a letter from *The Times of London* dated September, 1953. It was addressed to a Mrs. R. Hewitt of 3430 West 10th Street in Erie, PA., but the greeting referred to "Mr." Hewitt:

Dear Mr. Hewitt,

"Britain's Homage." This volume brings with it my sincere regards. I should be delighted to know from you that it has arrived safely.

Yours very truly, (an illegible first name) Astor, Chairman

Was this book sent to Mrs. Hewitt because she was the next of kin of one of those 28,000 Americans?

In preparing this Flashback I sent letters to all the "Hewitt's" listed in the Erie phone book asking if they knew of the Hewitt family that lived on West 10th Street more than fifty years ago. Did they know of a Hewitt who died in World War II? I have had no response to those letters.

When I told this story to an acquaintance of mine who lived in the northwestern part of Millcreek Township in the late 1950's, she did remember a family by that name that once lived "out by the airport". She believed the family had two sons (she had dated one of them) and that both had since moved to Ohio. Were these the sons of an Erie Hewitt who died in World War II? Was the name of a member of this family listed in the Roll of Honour that now rests in St. Paul's American Chapel? Were similar copies of this book also sent to other Erie families by *The Times of London*?

Perhaps someone reading this Flashback can tell us the rest of the story.

Epilogue – Part I

The mystery of the ownership of the book was resolved after the above Flashback was published. First I received a phone call from a Mr. Ted Loder who said his sister Rosina had been married for a short time to a Robert Hewitt who was killed during World War II. The "Mrs. R. Hewitt" to whom The Times of London addressed their letter was probably Rosina but he did not recall her ever having lived at the West 10th Street address to which the letter had been sent. A day or two later I received a call from a Mr. Ed Hewitt who told me he was Robert's brother and that yes, his brother had been married to a woman named Rosina. He went on to say that he had visited England after the war and had gone to visit the famous church of St. Paul's in London. While there a tour guide suggested he visit the American Chapel where he unexpectedly found his brother's name listed. He took a picture of that page in the Roll of Honour.

I concluded, therefore, that the deceased American to whose family the book had been sent was in fact Robert Hewitt of Erie. His name had actually been seen in the Roll of Honour at St. Paul's and his wife was, in fact, Mrs. R. Hewitt. Case closed.

Two days later, however, I received a call from a Mrs. Kathleen Hamilton who told me a different story. She knew of a young man named Donald Hewitt, the son of Mrs. Ruth Hewitt, who had been stationed in England and who was killed in the war. The family had lived in Union City at one time but had moved to 3430 West 10th Street in Erie, PA. So, there were two Hewitts from Erie among the 28,000 names in the Roll of Honour. Mrs. Hamilton also told me that John Hewitt, Donald's nephew, presently lived in Waterford.

Some weeks later I received a note from a Shirley Abbott of Erie who told me that her brother, Major Earl Abbott, had been stationed in England and was killed on January 24, 1945. Because she wondered if his name was also listed in the book in the American Chapel, she sent St. Paul's a copy of the Flashback and inquired if her brother's name was listed among those of the other Americans. It was.

The result of this Flashback, then, is that we now know for a fact that there are at least three Erie service men listed in the Role of Honour in London's St. Paul Cathedral, Donald and Robert Hewitt and Earl Abbott.

Epilogue – Part 2: A note to Jeff Pinski, *Erie Times-News* (April 1, 1996)

Dear Jeff:

I received a letter today from Mrs. Kathleen Hamilton, a lady who has done some research and has come up with the definitive solution to our "Flashback Mystery".

The soldier listed in the Roll of Honour and to whose family the book I wrote about is sent is undoubtedly Lt. Donald Hewitt of Union City. The son of Mr. and Mrs. Frank Hewitt, he graduated from Union City High School in June, 1941 and enlisted in the army the following February. He received his basic training at Ft. Bragg, N.C. and later transferred to Ft. Sill, Oklahoma where he graduated from Officer Training School as a second lieutenant. That same year on Christmas Eve he landed in Africa and a few months later landed with the American Forces in Sicily. It was during the Sicilian campaign that he received his first wounds and was awarded the Purple Heart.

The Hewitt family first received unofficial word of their son's death from a Red Cross worker in England. The young woman writing the letter had been Lt. Hewitt's girlfriend in England. She had learned of Donald's death through information from a wounded officer who had returned to England for hospitalization. The officer claimed he had seen Lt. Hewitt fall in action.

Shortly after the war Mrs. Hewitt (whose first name was Ruth) moved to 3430 West 10th Street in Erie. It was to that address that the book in my possession was sent and addressed to a "Mrs. R. Hewitt." The family now living at that address, Richard and Sarah Heilmann, confirm that they purchased the home from Mrs. Ruth Hewitt.

We know for a fact that Robert Hewitt who had also been stationed in England and was from Erie died in a bombing run over Germany in the early 1940's. His brother, Ed Hewitt, has told me that he was in the American Chapel in St. Paul's and took a picture of the page in the Roll of Honour in which his brother's name was listed. Mr. Hewitt also remembers seeing a copy of the book Britain's Homage to 28,000 American Dead that had been sent to his father back in the 1950's.

So the conclusion is that there were two Hewitts killed in action who had an Erie connection. One was Robert Hewitt, husband of Rosina Hewitt and brother of Ed Hewitt. The other was Lt. Donald Hewitt of Union City, the son of Mr. and Mrs. Frank (Ruth) Hewitt. And since we have verification that Mrs. Ruth Hewitt once lived at 3430 West 10th Street, the book in my possession is undoubtedly hers.

As I had mentioned to you earlier, I was going to donate the book to the Erie County Public Library. They would not accept it because of its poor condition (torn cover, water stained, several loose pages, etc.). Mrs. Hamilton has suggested that I contact Mr. John Hewitt of 1311 Lee Road in Waterford, Lt. Donald Hewitt's nephew, to see if he would be interested in having the book or if he would rather, I can give it to the Union City Museum.

Gino

Copy: Mrs. Kathleen Hamilton,
1321 Oakmont Ave., Erie, PA 16505

⇛ Different view of the "American Chapel" with the "Roll of Honour" containing the names of the 28,000 Americans who died during that war after having been stationed on British soil.

Photo courtesy of St. Paul's Cathedral.

A letter sent to the Times of London – April 8, 1996

Editor, The Times of London
Times Newspapers Limited
Virginia Street
London E1 9XT, England

Dir Sir or Madam:

Enclosed with this letter is a copy of an article that appeared in the Times-News Weekender of Erie, Pennsylvania on March 23, 1996. As you can see, the article deals with a book that was published by The London Times in 1952, a copy of which was sent to a Mrs. R. Hewitt in Erie, Pennsylvania in September 1953. A photo-copy of the letter is also enclosed.

The mystery referred to in the article has been solved. The "Mrs. R. Hewitt" to whom the book was sent was probably Mrs. Ruth Hewitt, the mother of Donald Hewitt. Mrs. Hewitt, now deceased, did in fact live at the address shown on your letter of 1953 and I have seen documents verifying that her son was stationed in England at the time of his death.

Strangely enough, another Hewitt family contacted me after the article was published to inform me that they too had a relative who had died in a bombing run over Germany. His name was Robert Hewitt and he too had been stationed in England. Mr. Ed Hewitt, brother of the deceased, was in London in 1989 and just happened by chance to go to St. Paul's on tour. A guide there suggested that since he was an American he ought to make it a point to see the American Chapel. He followed her advice whereupon he found his brother's name in the Roll of Honour. Mr. Hewitt also remembers his father having a copy of the book described in the article.

Thus, although the article solved the mystery of the family to whom the book was originally sent, we have learned there were two Hewitt's from Erie listed in the Roll of Honour.

I have given the tattered cloth bound volume of Britain's *Homage to 28,000 American Dead* to Lt. Donald Hewitt's surviving nephew. Mrs. R. Hewitt's book, therefore, is once again in the possession of the next of kin of one of those 28,000 Americans as was the intent of your publishing company.

Sincerely,
Gino J. Carlotti
Copy: Jeff Pinski, Editor of *The Times-News Weekender*

• • •

ARMED FORCES DAY TRIBUTE

War drew us from our homeland in the sunlit springtime of our
youth. Those who did not come back alive remain in perpetual
springtime-forever young. And a part of them is with us always.
– Arlington National Cemetery website – Author unknown

  The American Emblem atop the entrance gate
of the American Cemetery at Nettuno, Italy.

Last year on the day after Memorial Day, my wife Ann and I visited
the American cemetery in the small town of Nettuno 38 miles south of
Rome. We had been there several times during previous trips to Italy but
this visit was going to be special because we would be showing this beautiful place to our cousins Fred and Joan Prisco on this, their first trip
abroad.

Often called simply "The American Cemetery at Anzio", it is in fact
the place where 7,861 Americans who died in the Sicily-Anzio campaign of World War II are buried. It is a most beautiful, serene, and
impressive resting place. Again this time, as in each of our previous visits, we walked among the seemingly endless rows of white marble headstones engraved with name, rank, military unit, and home state of the
individuals buried there. The names were typically American – men and
women from all parts of the United States, soldiers and sailors of various
nationalities, ethnic backgrounds and religions. It was the resting place,
it seemed, for a generation of America's young.

෴ A general view of the American Cemetery near Anzio, Italy, and a detail of one of the 490 headstones of "unknown" members of the military buried here. This is where 7,861 Americans who served in the Sicily-Anzio campaign of World War II are buried. The main monument at the cemetery has a bronze plaque with words: "1941-1945 – In proud remebrace of the achievements of her sons, and in humble tribute to their sacrifices, this memorial has been erected by the United States of America." Inscribed on a marble wall at the memorial chapel are the names of another 3,095 membrs of the military who were counted as missing in action, or buried at sea, during the Sicily-Anzio campaign.

From time to time we came upon white marble crosses whose inscription read simply "Here rests in honored glory a comrade in arms known but to God". Occasionally we would also come across a grave with a bouquet of fresh flowers resting at the base of the headstone. Where had the flowers come from? Who still remembered the soldier or sailor buried there? What stories would these headstones tell if they could talk?

On this occasion, however, we had a new experience, one which personalized for us the loss this cemetery represented. As we were about to leave the grounds for our return to Rome, we stopped to visit the administration building adjacent to the main gate. While looking at the photographs and artifacts in this mini-museum we struck up a conversation with an elderly American lady from Indiana who told us a story we will never forget.

She was 72 years old, she said, and she and her sister were in Italy for the very first time to visit their father's grave. He had died on the beach at Anzio in 1944. She explained how they had arrived in Italy two days earlier – the first of their family to ever do so – to attend the previous day's official Memorial Day ceremonies. Today they were visiting their dad's grave for the last time before going back to their hotel to prepare for their return flight home.

With tears welling up in her eyes, she said she was sad because this was not only her first visit to the cemetery but it would undoubtedly be her last due to her advanced age. As a touching conclusion to her story, she told us what she and her sister had brought with them from home to plant at their father's headstone – a small tuft of grass from their mother's grave. In turn, they were taking back a handful of Italian soil to scatter at their mother's grave.

Every time we have visited this cemetery Ann and I have cried at its sadness and its beauty and this day was no different . . . we cried again.

Before leaving the Anzio Cemetery, cousin Fred and I picked up copies of the booklets that are on display in the Administration Building. The information contained in these publications lists the monuments and cemeteries that are maintained throughout the world by the American Battle Monuments Commission. It is information worth sharing.

There are 8 American cemeteries in Belgium, France and England with the remains of over 36,000 Americans who died in World War I. An additional 14 cemeteries hold the remains of 107,060 Americans who died in World War II. These are located in Belgium, England, France, Holland, Honolulu, Italy, Luxembourg, Republic of the Philippines, and Puerto Rico. Additionally there are memorials in New York City, Honolulu, and San Francisco commemorating the 78,976 service personnel who were listed as "missing in action" during the Second World War and whose bodies have never been recovered.

More recent additions to these war memorials are, of course, the Korean and Vietnam memorials on the Mall in Washington commemorating those who gave their lives in those conflicts: 35,516 in Korea and 58,198 in Vietnam. The 10,704 military personnel who were listed as "missing" in those two wars are remembered at special memorials in Honolulu, Hawaii. Soon there will be another memorial on the Mall to honor those who served in World War II. In fact, the ground breaking for this long over due memorial took place November 11, 2000.

So today as we observe Armed Forces Day and prepare for the upcoming Memorial day celebration, let us not forget those who have died, especially those who died in our lifetime and are buried on foreign soil. Let us hope and pray that we will never again have to establish another military cemetery anywhere in the world.

• • •

WHEN WE DRESSED FOR THE OCCASION

Last Sunday when I went to church I wore a pair of tennis shoes, khaki pants, and a V-neck sweater over an open neck sport shirt. Last Sunday my father turned over in his grave! He certainly would not have approved of my attire.

e⁀ Christmas Day 1941 and me with my new bike. As you can see, I was "all dressed up" with a white shirt and tie, a pullover sweater that my mother had knit by hand, heavy winter weight knickers and long socks. In the immediate background is the Cascade Foundry and further back is the smoke stack of the Continental Rubber Works. Notice that the street was not paved all the way to the curb thus exposing an edging of brick.

For as far back as I can remember my father never went to church, a funeral home, a meeting at his club, visiting in the homes of friends, or any "official" gathering without wearing a shirt and a tie. And if there had been a recent death in the family, even of a relative in Italy, the necktie he wore for the next several months would be black. He was a proud man with standards and one of those standards was: "If you're in mourning, wear black." It was not that he had an extensive wardrobe from which to choose, he was a blue collar laborer who wore work clothes on his job and in his garden but he believed that you honored certain events by dressing appropriately for them.

This fact of how the common man dressed more formally in years gone by was really brought to my attention when I viewed the nine-part series "Baseball" that ran on PBS television a short time ago. This excellent documentary on the history of our national sport showed a lot of old footage of baseball games at crowded ball parks in all the major league cities. In the shots of pre-World War II games, almost without exception, the men seen in the stands were wearing suits and ties.

My parents and my fiance, Ann Ferrare, at our friend Glorine Pizzo's wedding. My father was dressed as usual for this special occasion in his blue serge suit, white shirt and tie. Ann was one of Glorine's bridesmaids.

Was it that only professionals and business men went to ball games in those days? I don't think so. These were just average guys out for a sporting event. These were the same men seen wearing shirts, ties and hats in old news films and documentaries of the '20s, '30s and '40s and in pictures of bread lines during the Great Depression.

World War II seemed to be the turning point in men's fashions. In general men usually wore dress shirts before that time. These were white and always with long sleeves, even on the hottest summer days. Short-sleeved dress shirts? Unheard of. And every man had a blue serge suit which usually came with two pairs of pants. It was after the war that "sportswear" and informality became the rule of the day. Sport shirts intended to be worn open at the neck were introduced at about that time and they were revolutionary. In fact, when sport shirts first came on the scene most men wore them buttoned up to the neck as they had always done with their white dress shirts. Old habits don't change easily.

In time even my father began to ease up a bit. He began to wear sport shirts, some with short sleeves, and sweaters but the shirt and tie standard continued for the events he considered important enough to require more formal attire.

In summertime, regardless of the temperature, men and boys also always wore long pants, never shorts. Summer trousers might be a lighter weight cotton than usual or even summer weight wool, but they were always long. The wearing of shorts, except by little boys, was just un-American!

And men always wore undershirts. Always!

The story is told about the time Clark Gable removed his shirt in a scene with Claudette Colbert in the movie "It Happened One Night." He was wearing no undershirt. A shocking and daring thing to do, especially in the presence of a lady, and a flagrant disregard for the rules of how men dressed properly. The result? The sale of undershirts plummeted across America. The rules had suddenly been changed.

Here are some of those rules (mostly for teenage boys) that go back to the '40s and '50s:

- Rule #1 – If you wear buckle galoshes, never, buckle them. Wear them open. If possible, avoid wearing them at all.
- Rule #2 – Outerwear jackets and coats must always have the collars turned up even if it is not very cold.
- Rule #3 – Once you are out of grade school, you must never wear a hat or cap again. If you do wear a knit cap, wear it as far back on your head as the pull of gravity will permit and under no circumstances must you ever cover your ears.
- Rule #4 – If you wear a long sleeve shirt with neither a jacket nor a sweater over it, the sleeves must be unbuttoned and rolled up two times. Not one or three times but two times. Shirt tails are always tucked in.
- Rule #5 – Never wear a scarf. (Mothers hated this rule almost as much as the "no hat" rule.)
- Rule #6 – White socks are a must! Especially with loafers. Don't forget to place a penny in the instep strap of the shoes.
- Rule #7 – Never wear socks that are sheer such as those made of lisle or silk, heaven forbid! And only "old" men wear socks with "clocks" (long, thin, woven designs that ran up either side of the socks at the ankle). Argyles are acceptable, especially if you're kind of "preppie" in style. Knee-high stockings should be worn with knickers.
- Rule #8 – Sneakers must always be black and go up over the ankles. Also, they are to be worn *only* in the summer. Try as much as possible not to wear them on pavement because they wear out too fast on that hard a surface. Sneakers are OK to play in around the neighborhood, but regular shoes are better.
- Rule #9 – Don't ever buy high top boots unless they have a small knife pocket on the side. High tops are worn best with knickers. (Note: High top boots looked like something a lumberjack would wear. They came up over the calf of your leg. And the neat thing about them was that in the winter time, if you had high tops on your mother would allow you to go without galoshes.)
- Rule #10 – Avoid wearing corduroy pants as much as possible. They're too noisy when you walk.
- Rule #11 – Unless you are really poor, live on a farm or work in a factory, try never to wear overalls (known today as "jeans"!). They are so inexpensive that it is embarrassing to wear them.
- Rule #12 – Sleeves on sweaters should always be pushed up to just below the elbow.
- Rule #13 – Summer clothes, especially white shoes and straw hats, must never be worn before Decoration Day (Memorial Day) or after Labor Day. Temperature,

weather or comfort have nothing to do with it. It is the calendar that dictates when things are worn.

- Rule #14 – Never wear long underwear on gym day.
- Rule #15 – Keep your shoes shined.
- Rule #16 – Grooming rules: Hair should always be neatly combed and parted, preferably into a pompadour, and held in place with some type of hair cream. When it gets to the point that hair touches the back of your shirt collar it is definitely time for a hair cut. Hair should never touch your ears.

The Carlotti brothers, Egisto (seated) and Luigi, in a picture from the mid 1920's shortly after they arrived in the United States. Formal portraits such as this were taken by Italian imigrants at the Vagnarelli Studio to send back to Italy to show their families they had "arrived" and were doing well.

Last Sunday after Mass, dressed as I was, we went out for breakfast. A young man near us in the restaurant had his baseball cap on (backwards, of course) while he ate. He wore faded jeans and no socks and his shoes had apparently never been shined. The unbuttoned plaid shirt he wore over what appeared to be a white undershirt was not tucked into his trousers. His long hair hung loosely over his ears and collar. A small diamond earring glistened in the light. He was a nice looking young man and he seemed well-mannered as he quietly chatted with the young lady accompanying him. His appearance caused not a stir in the restaurant nor did it seem to draw undue attention from those around him. He was typically dressed for the '90s. In fact, he looked rather clean and well-groomed.

I wondered what my father would have thought of him.

• • •

Gaining a Family,
Its History & Traditions

ᥡᥡ The family of Francesco and Carmella Ferrare with their seven children (one more was born later). My father-in-law, Cudgie, is the tall young man in the back.

Italian families are usually thought of as being large extended groups with multi-generational levels of grandparents, sons and daughters, grandchildren, aunts, uncles, and cousins by the score, all of whom usually live in close proximity to each other. That was not the case in my life. During my childhood years my entire family had been limited to my parents, one aunt, one uncle and two cousins. What other relatives I had lived in Italy and I had never met them.

The size of my family changed, however, on April 7, 1956 when I married Ann Ferrare. Not only did I now have a wife, but I had acquired an entire clan of American relatives. Included were my in-laws, Cudgie and Martha Saglimbene Ferrare and Ann's sister Marie and brother Philip plus two grandfathers, eighteen aunts and uncles and seventeen first cousins. Martha's brother's family lived in Warren, Pennsylvania, as did her sister Columbia's family while her other sister, Rose, lived in Erie. In addition there were Cudgie's cousins and their families: the

Veshecco's, another large family, who lived in Erie and the Ferracio's who lived in Vandergrift.

From early in 1951 when Ann and I began dating I became immersed in the life of this typical Italian-American family. There was the annual Ferrare family picnic, the annual Ferrare/Ferracio family picnic, Grandpa Ferrare's birthday party every January, the family New Year's Eve party, and the trips to Warren and Vandergrift for other family gatherings. There were baptisms, confirmations, and high school graduations to celebrate and, for a few years, even a family bowling league. As the years passed there were anniversaries, weddings, more baptisms, and, of course, an occasional funeral.

This was a whole new world for me. Coming from a family of only seven people, I now ran into relatives no matter where I went and I soon discovered I had a lot of names to learn and people to sort out. Now let's see: Cudgie's brothers were John, Mike, Andy, and Jim and their wives were Lillian, Roseann, Christina, and Loretta. His sisters were Ange, Civillia, and Lucy and their husbands were Angelo Scalise, Arthur "Buster" Phillips, and John DeSanti. Martha's family consisted of her brother Philip, his wife Lena, and sisters Columbia and Rose. Columbia was married to Ralph Pasquino and Aunt Rosie was married to Clem Intrieri.

꒰꒱ The family of John and Domenica Saglimbene with their son and three daughters. My mother-in-law, Martha, is on the far left.

91

🔊 Ann and I on our wedding day April 7, 1956 with our parents.

Fortunately, none of these aunts and uncles had more than two children so learning the names of cousins was not too difficult: The Ferrare kids were Frank, Carmel, Carol, Billy, Jamie and Michael. Others were Tony Scalise, Joe and John DeSanti, and Bobby and Audrey Phillips. On the Saglimbene side there were Joan and Carol, Carolyn and Ralph Pasquino Jr. , and Rosemarie and Barbara Intrieri.

Once I had the names down the rest was easy. Now all I had to learn was the family history. This task was taken care of by just listening to the stories that were told and retold at all the family gatherings over the years. There was the story of how Grandpa

🔊 And here we are with Grandpa Ferrare at our wedding breakfast at the Calabrese Club on West 16th Street.

Ferrare first settled in the coal regions of Pennsylvania and how he and his sons worked in the mines around Reynoldsville and Byrndale. There were stories about their move to Erie and how their family of five sons and three daughters lived in "Little Italy" prior to and during the Depression. They talked of the various homes they lived in from time to time and the old neighbors and friends they used to have. They spoke of the good times and the hard times and of the places where they had worked over the years. They talked a lot about Griswold Manufacturing where all the Ferrare's had worked at one time or another and they talked about baseball, football, and especially bowling, the favorite family pass time. Grandpa Ferrare also spoke often of the Italian city of Troia in the province of Foggia where he and his wife Carmella had come from in the early 1900's.

In 1994 when Ann and I were visiting Italy we went to Foggia for one day and met with several Ferrare cousins. It was the first time anyone from the Erie Ferrare clan had met Italian cousins and it was a wonderful experience. We toured the small, ancient mountain top town, visited the church of St. John of God, Troia's patron saint, and had a wonderful lunch with several family members. It was during that lunch that we heard a story about the Pennsylvania coal mines that we will never forget. It was a story that even the Ferrare's in the United States had never heard.

It seems that in the early 1900's a number of men from Foggia emigrated to America and, like Grandpa Ferrare, ended up as miners in Pennsylvania. The story recounted how on one occasion a group of Foggiani (men from the Foggia region) were working deep in a mine shaft when they began to hear the tolling of a church bell. At first they continued working disregarding the ringing bell, but after some time one of the men said that the bell sounded like that of the church of St. John of God in their hometown. How could that be? Troia was thousands of miles away. They stopped working and listened more carefully. Yes, it did sound like their parish bell.

Driven by curiosity, excitement, and a little fear, the men decided to go up above ground to see where the sound was coming from. Upon exiting the mine, they heard nothing. The bell had stopped ringing. Then suddenly they heard another sound, a terrible sound, one that miners for all time have feared. The shaft they had just left collapsed. "And so", our cousins told us, "our men from Troia had been saved by St. John of God".

We now had a new story to add to the Ferrare legends.

This picture was taken in 1970 during my first trip to Italy where I met all my Italian relatives for the first time. That's me in the very back row with some (but not all!) of my cousins, their spouses, and several of their children.

There were other stories too: about Uncle Mike Ferrare, the first of the family to go to college, and his experiences playing football at Duquesne and about his days as a teacher and coach in the Erie City schools; about Uncle John DeSanti who spent nine years in the TB hospital up on Lake Pleasant Road in his successful battle against tuberculosis. They talked about Martha's winning the Erie televised women's bowling championship in 1956; about Ann and her father winning the city's 600-700 Club Mixed Doubles bowling tournament in 1964; and they reminisced about the many train excursions Cudgie organized for Erie bowlers to American Bowling Congress tournaments during the 40's and 50's. These and the tales of their childhood were the stuff that made family gatherings with the aunts and uncles interesting.

Now, fifty years after I first met Ann, we see how the family has grown. Grandpa Ferrare and his children are gone except for Uncle Jimmy and his wife Loretta and his sister Lucy . On the Saglimbene side only Aunt Rosie survives. But their vacant places have been filled by the next generation of Ferrare's and Saglimbene's and the children and grandchildren of the 17 first cousins. There is also a whole new series of names that have been added to the list. Now we are Carlotti's, Bucci's, Phillips', Scalise's, Campanelli's, Roscinski's, Karle's, Lasher's, O'Donnel's, Prisco's, and Simeral's.

⚜ The Carlotti family in Erie is not large, but it is growing. This is my cousin Carl and his wife Alice with their family. It was taken on New Year's day of 1998.

The old traditions, however, continue to this day. The Ferrare Family picnic is still held each year and the Saglimbene's have a reunion about every two years. A "Women's Club" of Ferrare aunts and cousins meets once a month, and some of the male members take part in an annual golf outing. For Ann and I, celebrations with Ann's sister Marie Bucci and her brother Philip are much more common. We spend the major holidays together in one house or another and we celebrate the birthdays of all our grandchildren throughout the year.

In all this time my original Carlotti family of seven has also grown. My cousin Ednamae Sabol, now deceased, had four children and three grandchildren. Cousin Carl has three children and and seven grandchildren and, of course, our son Rick has given us two grandchildren, Jessica and Michael. With this growth our list of last names has also become somewhat longer with the addition of Sabol, Emery, Polka, and Candela.

My perception of having come from a small family also changed dramatically in 1970 when, at the age of 38, I went to Italy for the first time. There I met a whole batch of relatives I had never met before: two uncles, seven aunts, and 18 first cousins. In addition there were spouses and countless grandchildren with a whole new roster of names to add to the list of cousins; Caciagli, Boldrini, Citi, Angiolini, and Boschi.

꩜ Me with all my Caciagli first cousins at a restaurant in Pontedera in May of
2000. This is the first time that all of my maternal grandfather's grandchildren were
in one room at the same time. The picture also included two Carlotti cousins.

It was the Ferrare family all over again!

So now I am no longer in a family of seven. I belong to two large
families with traditions and histories to pass on to the younger generations. This is, after all, what being a family is all about.

Hopefully, this and my previous 16 "Flashbacks" columns will
become part of that legacy.

• • •

43 YEARS OF PICNICS

Where did you spend the Fourth of July of 1962? How about Memorial Day 1974? Labor Day 1989? I can tell you exactly where my family and I were on each of those holidays and on each similar day for the past 43 years! We were at a picnic with the Pizzo and Squeglia families, and we will be with them again this year.

Let me explain.

When my wife, the former Ann Ferrare, and I were dating in high school, her very best friend was Glorine Battistelli. Glorine was dating Ben Pizzo and Glorine's cousin, Lorraine Ferri, was dating Dick Squeglia. The six of us together with Ben's friends (Al DiMatteo, Eddie Palotta, Dino Pezzato and Tom DiRienzo) and some of Ann and Glorine's Academy High School classmates (Audrey Farina, Donna Bartone, Marylou and Marilyn Meyers, Norma Robertson, Carmella Carciola, and Donna Brower among others) became a group whose friendship would span a lifetime.

In the 1950's we were probably referred to as "a gang" which in those days meant quite a different thing from what it means today. We were just a bunch of good kids who hung around together, went to school functions together and to the weekend dances at St. Joe's and the Y-ASTEC. We went to the downtown movies and we went to house parties. We summered on the beach and on almost any evening we ended up at either The Red Tower or the College Inn for hamburgers and cokes.

We drove cars that today would be considered classics. Mine was a red 1946 Chevrolet convertible. Yes, we were like something from the "Happy Days" TV show of later years: white socks, penny loafers, and DA haircuts. We jitter bugged and we slow danced. And practically all of us smoked. We were cool.

Time passed. We graduated from high school with some of us going on to college while others entered the world of work. One by one the guys went into the service and gradually upon our return the weddings began. Of course we all attended each other's weddings for in most cases we were in the bridal party. In fact, if you were to see the wedding photos of those years the cast of characters were practically interchangeable.

By the late 1950's we were starting our families. We lived in rented apartments for the first few years and eventually started buying homes. We continued to be friends and although we didn't go out as much as when we were single we did see each other as often as possible. For our social activities we now were going to church dances and dinners and family oriented events around town. We made the rounds to visit each other's homes at Christmas time and we frequently met for an evening of card playing at one house or another. Most of our activities were centered around our children.

And we started having picnics!

I don't recall exactly how it started but at some point in about 1956 or 1957 the suggestion was made that we have a picnic on Memorial day. Somebody volunteered their back yard as the site and a list was drawn up of who-would-make-what for the menu of the day. So we packed up the kids and went to spend the day with our friends. The kids loved it and so did the adults.

We decided that summer that since the Memorial Day picnic went so well we ought to do it again on the Fourth of July. That turned out

~ This picture was taken in 1953 at the Town Casino in Buffalo and it shows the three couples whose friendship began in high school and lasts to this very day.
- Front row from left: Glorine Battistelli, Ann Ferrare, Lorraine Ferri.
- Back row: Ben Pizzo, me, Dick Squeglia.

well too, so we decided to do it again on Labor Day. Thus, the three-pic-nics-a-year tradition was begun.

Three families (Carlotti, Pizzo, Squeglia) were the "core" for these triple celebrations, but others from our circle of friends would join us from time to time. Caroline and Al DiMatteo, Joann and Tom DiRienzo and Audrey and Jim Amidon, to name a few. As time passed, however, our families grew and as schedules and lives became more complicated it dwindled down to just the original three families getting together for these holiday picnics and that is how it has remained.

Over the years the number of people involved in these gatherings fluctuated. Sometimes Glorine's sisters and their husbands would join us (Lena and Pat Savelli and Mae and Tony DiBacco). Sometimes Lorraine's brother and his wife (Syl and Ada Gerbi) would come. When our parents were alive they would often join us too. Occasionally cousins such as Myra and Tony Vacanti and their daughters and the DiBacco twins and their husbands and children or some of the Squeglia clan would drop by for coffee and dessert. There were even times when visit-ing relatives from out of town would join us, such as some of Ben's fam-ily from California. Eventually two more Squeglia's, Madeline and Jerry, became permanent members of the picnic circuit.

❧ The same three couples in the 1970's at one of our picnics. This one was in Squeglia's back yard.

99

Over the years the very nature of our picnics changed as our children grew. They went from being "kiddie" oriented gatherings to adult affairs with teenagers huddled together off to the side somewhere. When the teenagers became young adults, the boyfriends and girlfriends started showing up. Now, with all the grandchildren, we are back to "kiddie" oriented picnics once again.

Because the Pizzo's and the Squeglia's lived on upper Maple street near Glenwood Park, picnics in their yards included a walk to the zoo right after lunch. This was only for the dads with all the kids in tow while the women folk cleaned up. The usual Memorial Day activity was an afternoon stroll through the Erie Cemetery reading old tombstones and looking for the graves of well known Erieites, again with just dads and kids. And of course, no Fourth of July event could pass without sparklers for the kids as soon as the sun went down.

As we original six organizers age, we have begun to occasionally pass the responsibilities for hosting the picnics on to our children. They have yards of their own now. But we are still the main planners: will it be a breakfast menu at noon with steaks on the grill for supper or should we go with a roast on the spit for lunch with hot dogs and hamburgers in the evening? And what should all the side dishes be? Who will bring the desserts?

Making these decisions is important and we are not yet ready to pass that task entirely on to the younger generation, for planning a picnic has become an event in itself. It is done now by the three couples over a Friday night dinner where deciding the menu becomes as serious a matter as a meeting of the OPEC nations setting the price of world crude.

As evening falls and another picnic is about to end, the last thing we have to do is evaluate the day. I have appointed myself the official

The "head cook" is about to slice the roast at a picnic in our back yard when we lived at 1139 West 24th Street. Sitting at the table are Ben Pizzo and Mark Squeglia on the left and Stephen Pizzo and Lorraine Squeglia on the right.

100

judge and have established the "Carlotti Point System" to determine the official rating of picnics on a scale of 1 to 10. If it rains on Pizzo's picnic, for example, they lose points. If it takes too long for the charcoal to heat up at the Squeglia picnic the rating drops. If the corn was not as tasty as we had hoped it would be, points are lost. Even the condition of the host's lawn is considered.

Earning a score of 10 is next to impossible unless, of course, the picnic is in our yard! One year our event went to an unprecedented eleven! Nobody (including my own wife!) agrees with my ratings but as with any good official, my decisions stand no matter who finds fault with them! When it comes to the "Carlotti Point System" my motto is: "Always challenged but never changed!"

It has been 43 years now that we have been together and we would not have it any other way. Friendships such as these are more valuable than gold.

Now, let's see. Whose turn is it to have this Memorial Day?

GLOSSARY

For those of you who were not around in the 50's, I will have to explain some terms used in this Flashback.

❶ **D.A. haircut** – Boys would comb their hair back on the sides so that it would meet in the back of the head forming what looked like the tail end of a duck. Thus the term "Duck's A _ _" usually referred to simply by the letters D.A.

❷ **St. Joe's** – St. Joseph Catholic Church on 25th and Sassafras sponsored weekly dances in the gym of the old school. Everybody went stag but it was a great place to meet friends and classmates and especially for boys to meet girls, and girls to meet boys. It was very busy on the nights of football games.

❸ **Y-ASTEC** – Another weekly teen dance. Sponsored by the downtown YMCA. The name was made up of the first letter of each of the city's major high schools – Academy, Strong Vincent, Tech, East, Cathedral Prep. A somewhat different crowd than went to St. Joe's but still a good place to meet people.

❹ **The Red Tower** – A hamburger restaurant out on West 26th Street near Pittsburgh Ave. Had a jukebox and dance floor. Long before fast food restaurants came along.

❺ **College Inn** – Another restaurant that was one or two notches up in quality and atmosphere from the Red Tower. Located on Glenwood Park Avenue near 38th Street at about where the Country Fair Store is now located. "The" place to go after a dance. Also had a jukebox and dance floor.

• • •

BACK TO OUR ROOTS

In September of 1998 my cousin Carl and I went to Italy for a ten day visit with our relatives. The purpose of the trip was twofold: first to attend a cousin's 50th Wedding Anniversary celebration, and the second to show Carl, who would be seeing Italy for the first time, the birthplace of our fathers, Egisto and Luigi Carlotti.

We departed from Erie on a Friday flying to Pisa by way of Pittsburgh, Philadelphia and Rome. By late Saturday afternoon we were in my cousin Renza's house in Pontedera, a small town near Pisa. On the following day we were to be part of two family celebrations. The first was the baptism of Renza's and Giuliano's month old granddaughter at the 10:00 o'clock Sunday morning Mass. The other was the golden wedding anniversary dinner to which we had been invited.

The anniversary party was wonderful. All of my cousins and Zia Beppa, my 94 year old aunt, were there making it truly a Caciagli family reunion. Although this was my mother's side of the family, Carl was welcome by all with open arms and the traditional kisses on both cheeks! And the meal, what can I say, it was fantastic! It began at 12:30 and did not end until 5:00 pm. Counting the various *antipasti* (appetizers) there were 16 different items served with endless bottles of wine and bottled mineral water culminating with two desserts and glasses of champagne.

We did not have supper that evening.

Carl was impressed with the whole day not so much by the endless food and drink, but rather with the warmth and friendliness of the people who were there. This was his first experience amidst a large family gathering celebrating in a typically Italian manner, joyous, loving, open and welcoming.

The highlight of the trip was the afternoon we spent in Bientina, a town about the size of Girard just a short drive from where we were staying in Pontedera. Our cousin Ubaldo Carlotti escorted us to the house in the outskirts of town where our fathers were born in the late 1800's. Renovated many times over the years, the house still stands amidst the fields of rich soil where our family farmed for countless generations. We

❧ Me and Carl in the Piazza dei Miracoli in Pisa during our trip there in 1998. In the background you can see the famous Leaning Tower and right next to it is "Il Duomo di Pisa", Pisa's Cathedral. The front of the church was covered in scaffolding as it was being cleaned and refurbished in preparation for the Holy Year that would be celebrated throughout Italy in the year 2000.

were truly standing on the ground from which our family originated. We also visited the main square in town where the church of Santa Maria Assunta (the church of the Assumption of Mary) is located. It was in that church where our fathers, our grandparents and our great grandparents were baptized, where they made their first communion, where they were confirmed, married and from which they were buried. While kneeling in that beautiful old church in silence and in darkness on a beautiful autumn evening we seemed to be surrounded with the spirits of our ancestors. It was a wonderful feeling of comfort and peace.

Ubaldo also took us to the cemetery to see the tombstones of our grandparents and those of all our aunts and uncles. I say "tombstones" rather than "graves" because the graves have been recycled for use by others. All that remains are the headstones that now line the cemetery walls, The oldest of these, of course, were those of our grandfather Carlo, 1857-1919, and our grandmother Teresa, 1862-1929. To me and to Carl it was like being in the presence of the *nonni* (grandparents) we never knew.

From there we went to meet Tiziano, a man Carl had not seen in 55 years.

During World War II our aunt Maria's son, Tiziano Nieri, was captured by the Americans in North Africa in 1943. After being transferred to several prison of war camps in Europe and the United State, he was ultimately sent to a camp in Summerville, New Jersey. In the summer of '43 Carl, then 16 years old, together with his father and my father went by train to Summerville to visit Tiziano.

✿ This picture, taken in Buti, Italy in the summer of 1998, is of my cousin Carl (on the left) meeting our cousin Tiziano Nieri, whom he had not seen in 55 years. They first met in 1944 when Carl was sixteen years old and Tiziano was an American prisoner of war at a camp in Summerville, New Jersey. Standing off to the right and obviously enjoying this momentous reunion is another cousin, Ubaldo Carlotti of Bientina, Italy.

This meeting in Bientina would be only the second time these two men would have seen each other and their first meeting in more than half a century. It was a beautiful moment and it meant a great deal to both of them.

While having some light refreshments in Tiziano's home, he brought out the letters and pictures that Carl, his sister Ednamae, and I had sent to him during his stay in Summerville. He told us how much those letters had meant to him at that time and how he treasures them still. Their value to him was obvious in the way he handled them and how he stored them in plastic envelopes which were kept in a special box in a dresser drawer. He spoke, too, of the fond memories he has of those many months he spent in the United States; of how well treated he and his fellow prisoners were; of the many kindnesses shown them by American civilians and military personnel; and of how fortunate he was to have been captured by the Americans. He also remembered well that visit from his two uncles and his young cousin. That day in Bientina made the whole trip worthwhile.

But no trip to Italy would be complete without seeing some of the major sights. For Carl, especially, visiting these historic places and seeing some of the wonders Italy has to offer was an important part of appreciating where our family came from and who we were. So we spent some time in three magnificent historic cities: Florence, Pisa and Rome.

Our first day trip was to Florence.

To walk the streets of that ancient city and to see the palazzi (palaces), the churches, the museums, the monuments and statues that are known and revered the world over is a thrill that is almost beyond description. And to think that these sights, this culture, existed before America was even born boggles the mind.

The Piazza della Signoria, the main square in Florence, was as always, filled with tourists taking pictures of the Palazzo Vecchio (the Old Palace) with its famous statue of David standing at the entrance. Although we were in the crowded center of one of Italy's most famous cities, the voices around us were not speaking Italian. We were hearing Japanese, German, English, and other languages we did not recognize.

The same was true as we walked across Ponte Vecchio (the Old Bridge) that spans the Arno River. Because they lived on one side of the Arno river and worked in the city center on the other side, the Medici family built this covered bridge in 1345 so they could more easily reach their offices in what is now the Uffizzi galleries. Lined with numerous shops of Florentine jewelers and silversmiths, Ponte Vecchio is today more than just a mere bridge: it is a very chique and expensive shopping center specializing in jewelry of Italian gold. The shop windows are dazzling!

After a morning of sightseeing we went to McDonald's for lunch. It looked the same as the McDonald's at home, golden arches and all. It even smelled the same. But did it taste the same? The answer to that is "Yes, sort of." My Big Mac and fries were good but I would swear they used a slightly different seasoning. There was also another minor difference: we could have either ketchup or mayonnaise in which to dunk our fries.

Our next day trip was to Pisa to see the Leaning Tower. What most people don't realize, having only seen photographs of the tower, is that it does not stand alone in some open space. In fact, it is one of four buildings making up the complex of the Piazza Dei Miracoli (Miracle Square): Il Duomo (The Cathedral), the baptistery, a walled cemetery, and the cathedral's bell tower, the Leaning Tower.

Like all tourists, we had a picture taken of us with the tower in the background and we visited the beautiful cathedral and the baptistery. Unlike most tourists, however, we also entered the cemetery to view the graves of antiquity in the floors and walls of the structure. Most tourists also do not know that all the soil in the grassy area within those cemetery walls is soil brought back to Pisa as ballast in ancient ships returning from the Holy Land at the time of the Crusades.

How often our parents had spoken of the beauty of this place. How proud they were to have been born and raised in this province of Pisa. That famous tower was "their tower" to which they always referred simply as "il campanile", the bell tower.

Could Carl and I now consider that "our tower" too?

The final leg of our journey took us to Aprilia about an hour's drive from Rome. It is a modern city built by Mussolini before World War II. It was almost totally destroyed in 1944 during the nearby battle at Anzio between the Allied forces and the German army. The only scars of that conflict still evident in the city are the bullet holes that pierce the bronze statue of St. Michael as it stands in the town square at the entrance to the church of St. Michael.

It was from Aprilia that we began several day trips to visit the "three Romes": modern Rome with the beautiful glass and marble office buildings befitting a world capitol and commercial center; ancient Rome with the ruins of the Circus Maximus, the Coliseum, the Roman Forum, and the aqueducts; and finally, to religious Rome, the center of the Roman Catholic Church at the Vatican.

We visited the church of San Pietro in Vincoli (St. Peter in Chains) to see Michelangelo's magnificent statue of Moses and then to St. Peter's Basilica. We crossed the basilica's marvelous square with its famous circular colonnade before entering the church itself. What an experience! With Michelangelo's Pieta, the main altar with its Bernini columns, the paintings, the statuary, the mosaics, and the immensity of it all, St. Peter's is almost more than one can handle! It is breathtaking, to say the least. Carl was thrilled.

Unfortunately, at the time that we were there the facade of St. Peter's and those of most of the major churches throughout Italy were covered in scaffolding as they were being cleaned and repaired for the massive invasion of tourists expected to arrive to celebrate the millennium in the year 2000. Even though some picture postcard vistas were temporarily blocked because of this work, there was still ample opportunity to be moved and thrilled by the sights and sounds of Rome. Goose bumps still happened!

As we left Rome for a short ride to Castel Gandolfo, the Pope's summer residence on Lake Gandolfo, we traveled on the ancient Via Appia (the Appian Way). To see the ancient walls, the entrances to historic villas of early Roman times, the ruins of monuments to past emperors, entrances to various parts of the catacombs, and segments of the aqueducts that brought water from the mountains into the city, was like traveling back in time.

Our final stop was to the town of Nettuno (Neptune) to visit the American Cemetery at Anzio.

The huge bronze American Eagle emblem over the entrance to this World War II cemetery is inscribed with the words "Sicily-Rome-American Cemetery and Memorial." Beyond its walls are 7,861 marble crosses and Stars of David marking the graves of American service men and women who died in the battle to liberate Italy of German control. The shrubs and trees are beautifully maintained and the lawn is better than any fairway on the finest American golf course. There are formal gardens and reflecting pools and in the center of it all a beautiful monument with this inscription:

> 1941
> •
> 1945
>
> In proud remembrance of the achievements of their sons and in humble tribute to their sacrifices this memorial has been erected by the United States of America.

Carl with cousins Ugo and Alberto at the entrance to the beautiful American Cemetery at Anzio in the small town of Nettuno, 35 miles south of Rome.

There were four of us on this sightseeing trip and after we had walked through the front gates we separated with each of us strolling alone and in silence for 45 minutes through rows upon rows of graves. Name, rank, unit, date of death, home state. Name, rank, unit, date of death, home state. Name, rank, unit... And every so often one marker would say simply: "Here lies in honored glory a comrade in arms known but to God."

At two of the graves, one of a boy from Pennsylvania, there were bouquets of fresh flowers. Who brought them? Was a family member visiting from the states? Was it an Italian who had met the young man and remembers him still after more than 50 years? What interesting stories those flowers would tell if they could talk.

This was not my first visit to Anzio but as happened in all previous visits, the beauty of the place, its silence, its sadness, touched me deeply. I cried.

This was a wonderful trip that provided us with memories to last a lifetime: memories of wonderful gatherings with family and friends; memories of the family stories that have been told and retold for generations; memories of the beautiful places we visited and the marvelous things that we saw. Yes, we will even remember how delicious the food and wine were. But most important of all, we will remember being at the very place where our family began in the country whose culture is our cherished heritage.

Carl and I were blessed with the opportunity of a lifetime, the opportunity to proudly return to our roots.

•••